THE WAY OF THE FIGHTER:
BRUCE LEE'S TRUE STORY

His goal? To be the first oriental superstar, to raise his people to a place of honor in the world, to give his family a good life—and, most of all, to be respected as a man.

His genius? He was the deadliest Kung Fu fighter, improving the ancient art into Jeet Kune Do, the Way of the Intercepting Fist. He did away with the classic stances, developing a technique of moving with the action, adapting to each situation.

Follow his rise to fame and fortune, learn the philosophy and the methods he developed, and share his deepest feelings as Linda, his wife and closest friend, remembers his life and tragic death in

BRUCE LEE:
THE MAN ONLY I KNEW

BRUCE LEE:
THE MAN ONLY I KNEW

by Linda Lee

WARNER PAPERBACK LIBRARY

A Warner Communications Company

WARNER PAPERBACK LIBRARY EDITION
First Printing: April, 1975
Second Printing: June, 1975
Third Printing: August, 1975

This Warner Paperback Library Edition is published by arrangement
with W.H. Allen & Co. Ltd. a division of Howard & Wyndham Ltd.

Warner Paperback Library is a division of Warner Books, Inc.,
75 Rockefeller Plaza, New York, N.Y. 10019.

 A Warner Communications Company

Printed in the United States of America

Not associated with Warner Press, Inc. of Anderson, Indiana

To our children—the two people who brought to Bruce more joy, more love, and more fulfillment than all the wings of fame and fortune. I hope they know he loved them as life itself. This book is dedicated to Brandon and Shannon, that they might know the rich legacy which is theirs alone.

—Linda Lee

ACKNOWLEDGEMENT

I would like to express my indebtedness to those who have helped and supported me in the writing of this book, and who have contributed their time and effort and their memories: To *Max Caulfield* and *Alan Shadrake*, without whom this book would not have been written. And to the following friends and family whose hearts were truly touched by Bruce: *Grace Lee*, his mother; *Robert Li*, his brother; *Phoebe Ho*, his sister; *Vivian McCulloch*, my mother; *Adrian Marshall*, our lawyer; *Taky Kimura, Dan Inosanto, Ted Wong, Herb Jackson, Peter Chin* and *James Coburn*, his students; *Jhoon Rhee and Al Dacascos*, Bruce's fellow martial artists; *Fred Weintraub*, producer of *Enter The Dragon;* and *Jim Grunwald*, photography.

ONE

It was around noon on July 20, 1973 when I left our Kowloon house to lunch with a girl friend. Bruce was in his study at the time dictating to his secretary. His study, of course, was the most important room in the house. It was where he kept all his books—he had a magnificent library of several thousand volumes dealing with every conceivable aspect of physical combat, ancient and modern, as well as with weapons of all kinds, calisthenics, sports, film-making and both Oriental and Western philosophy—though the focal point was probably the big desk with its telephones. Bruce practically lived in his study. He would lock himself away for hours to read and study; he conducted most of his business from his desk; worked on the scripts of *The Way of the Dragon* and *Enter the Dragon*, his classic presentations of the martial art of kung fu.

He was his usual industrious, intense self when I left him. Through the veranda window he could see our garden which had been laid out in the Japanese style with wandering paths and a goldfish pond with a little bridge across it and a stream which meandered in and out of the trees and through the Korean grass. By Hong Kong standards we had a lavish place; an eleven-roomed villa with spacious grounds surrounded by an eight-foot-high stone wall and a large wrought-iron gate at the front entrance. We had not consciously set out to live in such style but Hong Kong is cramped and overcrowded. Most people live in small flats, stacked one on top of the other, and there are only a few residential properties available, all rather large and expensive. Bruce, however, desperately needed to escape the noises of every-

9

day living and the shouts of children to work and study, so we were fortunate to find a residential property for sale.

Bruce told me that producer Raymond Chow of Golden Harvest was coming over that afternoon to talk about script ideas for *The Game of Death*. Most of the action scenes for this film had been shot, including a spectacular encounter between Bruce who was only five foot seven and Kareem Abdul Jabbar, the American basketball star who is seven foot two; as yet, though, they had neither a finished plot nor script (the film is still uncompleted). Bruce said that he and Chow would probably dine later with George Lazenby, whom Raymond hoped to co-star; Lazenby is the actor who took over the James Bond role when Sean Connery quit.

That was the last conversation I ever had with my husband.

I returned home about four o'clock and spent the evening doing my physical exercises and watching TV in Bruce's study with my two children, Brandon and Shannon. I remember thinking it a little odd that Bruce hadn't phoned for although he had told me he would probably be dining out he usually called to confirm arrangements. Instead, sometime around ten o'clock, Raymond Chow called; there was a note of urgency in his voice.

'Would you go to the Queen Elizabeth hospital right away, Linda,' he said. 'Bruce is on the way there—in an ambulance.'

'What's the matter?' I demanded.

'I don't know—something like the last time.'

I was terribly concerned but I cannot say that I was shocked because Bruce was always involved in the unexpected. Besides, we had been through many crises before. I had learned to flow with him in the current of his chosen life-style, to live each moment for itself. He was constantly phoning and saying, 'Meet me in fifteen minutes' or 'Listen, Linda, I've just had the most fantastic news!' Even before we were married, I told him, 'You know, Bruce, I just can't keep up with you.' Only

10

three months earlier, on May 10, he had collapsed at the studios and been rushed to the hospital but had quickly recovered. Later medical tests in Los Angeles had disclosed nothing wrong with him; the doctors, indeed, had assured him that he was as fit as an eighteen-year-old.

I arrived at the hospital about fifteen minutes before the ambulance but at first it seemed as if there had been some mistake because nobody knew anything about Bruce being brought in and the man at the desk even suggested, 'Somebody must have been joking—we don't know anything about it.' I hung on, however, and eventually the ambulance arrived. He was apparently unconscious but I could not find out exactly what was happening because the doctors were swarming around him. He was carried into an emergency ward and a team began massaging his heart. It never occurred to me that he might die—might even be dead—probably because I thought that once he had arrived in the hospital everything was going to be all right.

Bruce had talked about death more than once in recent months. He was certainly convinced that he would never live to be an old man (nor, indeed, did he want to—he told his brother Robert that he hated the idea of growing old and weak).

'I won't live as long as you,' he told me one day.

'Why would you think that?' I asked. 'You're a lot healthier than I am and in far better condition, for heaven's sake.'

"I don't really know. The fact is I don't know how long I can keep this up.'

Bruce, in so many senses the very essence of physical fitness, a man almost totally absorbed with his body and extraordinary abilities, subconsciously felt (as have other men who die young) a strong sense of urgency to get a great many things done in a short space of time. He was under the severest pressures. A unique artist and a legend in his own lifetime—karate experts everywhere recognized him as the Galileo of the martial arts, the deadliest *fighting* exponent of unarmed combat in the

11

world—he was well on the way to becoming the highest-paid actor in films. He was the first Oriental superstar to bridge the chasm between East and West, to contradict the outrageous stereotypes represented on film and TV by such 'Chinese' figures as Charlie Chan and Dr. Fu Manchu and had, therefore, become a hero to millions in Southeast Asia who identified with him and saw him as their champion. A lethal whirlwind of flying fists and blurring legs, his magic kick had taken western audiences by storm as he spectacularly revealed mysteries known only to the Chinese for centuries. Singlehandedly, he had made the whole world conscious of kung fu.

Suddenly, Bruce found himself in urgent demand by film-makers everywhere. Phil Ochs, a member of the legendary New York folk music circle of the early sixties that once included Bob Dylan has described how he 'sat entranced' for three hours when he first stumbled across two of Bruce's films in the Philippines. 'I could hardly believe my eyes. I had seen the Japanese samurai movies, but was not prepared for what was to come. The stories were simplistic and based mainly on revenge. They always involved fighting schools and a revered master teacher: "I will teach you to be the best fighters in the world, but you must never use it to harm anyone unless absolutely necessary." Near the beginning is the act of outrage; the insults of a rival school, the poisoning of a master, the murder of a loved one. Lee, the hero, the best fighter, demands vengeance and is always restrained until he can hold himself in no longer. Then follows the most exciting action ever filmed for the screen. One man against fifty with no weapons. He begins to wade his way through the lesser villains with karate chops; his fists, his elbows, his feet; there are no camera tricks. The audience is hysterical, clapping, cheering, sometimes leaping to their feet. When he gets to the major villains it becomes a dance of extraordinary beauty (one reviewer said that Lee made Rudolf Nureyev look like a truck driver). It is not the vulgarity of James Arness pistol-whipping a stubbled, drunken stage robber; it is not the ingenious devices of James Bond coming to the rescue, nor the ham-fisted John Wayne slugging it out in the saloon over crumbling tables and paper-thin imitation glass. It is the science of the body taken to its highest form; and the violence no matter how outrageous, is always strangely purifying. As important as the action is the face and mind of Bruce Lee. The expressions on his face as he psyches out his opponents are beyond description; at times he is lost in ecstasy, almost sexual, and when he strikes, the force of the blow is continued by his mind and the look of concentration and satisfaction is devastating.'

The offers poured in. Run Run Shaw, the Hong Kong millionaire film producer who only three years earlier had offered him a ridiculously small amount for a film, now offered him £100,000 a film and when Bruce brushed it aside, sent him a signed open contract with a request that he fill in his own figures. Sophia Loren's producer-husband, Carlo Ponti, was only one of several Italian film-makers who cabled him fantastic offers. Warner Brothers had already spent close to a million making *Enter the Dragon*—then still to be released—and urgently intended to follow it up. As the craze for kung fu movies swept the world, Bruce found himself the hottest property in show business, a greater box office star than Steve McQueen. Simultaneously his problems multiplied. Could he widen his international appeal without destroying his popularity on the Mandarin circuit? Could he inject greater quality into his films without destroying their essence; perhaps help to educate the millions with whom he shared ethnic and cultural backgrounds; teach martial artists everywhere the need to find their own truth?

He was beset, too, by sheer physical day-to-day problems. Working and living conditions in Hong Kong are scarcely ideal. Hong Kong can be a pretty rough place; there were always people challenging him to fight on the streets, hoping to boast that they had beaten the master. He could never escape from business associates; from people wanting to make deals or thrusting contracts literally under his nose; from the press, radio, TV; from autograph-hunters mobbing him whenever he appeared. In Hollywood, it would have been easy to get out of town on weekends or relax for a day or two in the country but in cramped Hong Kong it was out of the question. By nature and temperament, too, Bruce had a craving for high-wire living. He was a highly-strung person and under certain conditions could even become quite excitable. When he was a child, his family had nicknamed him (in Chinese) 'Never sits still'. He knew he needed to relax but somehow there was always something that had to be attended to immediately; there never was time. Throughout early 1973, Bruce was constantly on the go—arguing over scripts or talking for hours on the telephone or holding conferences; towards the end he had so many problems in his head that he could not sleep.

The strains had dramatically intensified once he decided to make *Enter the Dragon*, his first big international picture. He was nervous and apprehensive about tackling it; there were major problems with the script and complications arising from the differences between Hollywood and Hong Kong movie production values. It was a time, too, when he was suffering many emotional ups and downs. Bruce was always a very emotionally involved person—one of the reasons for his success —but the pressures at the time made him especially moody.

I had tried to tell him that there was no longer any need for him to work so hard; that his career was now running along the right lines and the future was assured; besides, the important thing was that the four of us should be together, that as long as we had each other, everything was fine. Yet it was not easy for Bruce to forget the relatively lean times we had earlier experienced and he was determined that the children and I should never again have to face anything like financial uncertainty. Once or twice he talked about 'in case anything happens to me' for he was aware that everything depended on a fragile foundation; his continued physical

14

fitness. In 1970, he had suffered a terrific shock. Few men, I suppose, have ever sought to discipline their bodies with such dedication as Bruce; there was hardly an inch of his lithe, beautifully-balanced frame, with its steel-like muscles, which he had not subjected to fierce and repeated exercises. Weight-lifting was normally not too important to him; he merely used weights for a few specific areas of his body to develop power rather than large muscles. But one morning he decided to experiment with a 125-pound weight, placing the weight on his shoulders and bending over from the waist while keeping his back straight.

I don't think he fully appreciated how strenuous this exercise is for he suddenly felt a terrible pain in the lower part of his back. The doctor told him he had damaged a sacral nerve and would never do his kung fu kick again. But short of having both his legs chopped off, Bruce could never reconcile himself to giving up kung fu. The doctor warned him it meant lying on his back for a long time. Normally telling Bruce even to take it easy was like trying to tell a grasshopper not to jump but when he set his mind to it, he could do anything. He stayed in bed for three months—enduring a period of great mental and physical pain, stress and financial problems. Altogether it was more than six months before he could resume even light training. But even during his recuperation his mind remained extraordinarily active. These months were spent setting down notes on the martial way. I am presently compiling these and will work them into a separate book to be published at a later date. It was possibly the blackest period in his life; the only time, I think, when his soaring spirit felt the full weight of the world but the lessons were not lost on him—and if he ever felt inclined to forget them, a twinge of pain reminded him.

Nevertheless, he still continued to live life with his usual zest and energy, and yet I sensed that the tensions and pressures were reaching their peak. Had he lived, I'm sure he would have found an inner contentment based on his philosophy of life. I believe he sensed it

Linda Lee, mother and author, with Brandon and Shannon.

himself, not simply that he would die, but that a major turning point was imminent. He loved the song *And When I Die* and the line which goes 'If it's peace you find dying, well then let the time be near'. Once or twice he mentioned, 'Maybe that's the only place where I'll find peace.' John Saxon, who starred with him in *Enter the Dragon*, says that Bruce was really shaken by his collapse in May and while awaiting the outcome of the Los Angeles tests said to him, 'Maybe if they don't work out, there isn't going to be a Bruce Lee.'

And so now, for the second time within three months, I found myself in a bare hospital ward watching a team of doctors working on him. Strangely, I felt almost no emotion; I suppose I was too numbed by shock. Grief, despair, the sense of loss—all these were to come later. Besides I believed Bruce was merely unconscious for nobody had told me he was already dead. After a minute or so, they suddenly rushed Bruce upstairs and we all had to run along a corridor to an intensive care unit. Here they injected drugs directly into Bruce's heart and applied electric shock treatment. Somebody tried to pull me away saying, 'I don't think you want to see this,' but I struggled free and insisted, 'Leave me alone—I want to know what's happening.' Then I noticed that the machine recording Bruce's heartbeat had stopped beeping, which indicated that he was not alive and I suddenly realized what had really happened. Yet I still refused to believe the unbelievable; I was convinced that Bruce would always win through. He had so much life and vitality; he generated so much inner force and had such control over his mind and his body; he had fought his way out of so many adverse situations and survived so much. I simply could not accept that he would not win through as he had in May.

When I asked the doctor, I did not use the word *dead*; it was not a word I could use about Bruce. Instead, I asked, 'Is he alive?' The doctor shook his head.

I can't remember much about what happened after that. I know I wandered along the corridor by myself for a while. Then I vaguely remember Raymond Chow telephoning his wife, asking her to come and pick us up. I remember the head of the medical team asking me if I wanted an autopsy and replying, 'Yes, I want to know how he died.' I remember the reporters swarming in the hospital entrance and the flash of photographers' bulbs. I insisted on going back to see Bruce one more time to make sure for myself that he was gone. And as I now reflect, it was at that point (when the life force had barely been extinguished) that I felt an incredible strength surge through my body and spirit. No panic or despair. The determination and courage of Bruce himself passed to me. In a flash I knew what lay ahead and how I should deal with everything in the best possible way for Bruce, Brandon and Shannon.

It was only much later that I became conscious that, because he was an almost mythical figure, Bruce's death would stun millions all over the world. Yet even I could hardly have guessed that more than one year after his death his name would, if anything, be even greater and more widely known than when he was alive; that his films would be revived again and again; that like earlier great screen figures such as Rudolph Valentino and James Dean who had died before their time, he would become the nexus of a world cult.

TWO

I first saw Bruce Lee in the spring of 1963 while I was attending Garfield High School in Seattle. Bruce, who was then a philosophy major at the University of Washington used to come to our school to lecture in Oriental philosophy and I often saw him walking around the halls, always with a girl friend. I'm told that since he was fifteen, Bruce had never had any trouble dating girls.

I spoke to him for the first time when a Chinese girl friend of mine who was taking lessons in the martial arts brought me along one evening to Bruce's little basement club in Seattle's Chinatown—a dingy little cell no more than twenty feet by twenty feet. He called this the Jun Fan Gung Fu Institute because his Chinese name was Lee Jun Fan and because he pronounced kung fu in the Cantonese style, gung fu. He had begun by giving lessons in parking lots, empty buildings, school gyms or fraternity houses. Then realizing the potential for martial arts in America—karate was just beginning to catch on—he had decided to open the club. He planned to open a chain of gung fu schools throughout the United States; this idea he eventually found impracticable because neither his methods nor the philosophy that lay behind them could be taught en masse. He made no attempt to advertise the Institute and there wasn't even a sign outside the door. He hoped that the school's reputation and the value of his instruction would be spread by word of mouth. He wanted to teach people who, apart from a genuine interest in the martial arts, were prepared to grapple with the philosophical ideas underlying them.

I suppose the first thing I noticed about Bruce was the immense command he had of his body; the amazing reflexes that seemed more feline than human; the ability to perform quite astonishing feats of strength such as doing push-ups on ONE FINGER! Nothing, of course, had prepared me for the sheer impact of his personality.

Taky Kimura, a Japanese-American and Bruce's friend and assistant at the club, has described it as 'like an electrifying force that drew you to him. He was an outstanding person in a crowd . . . He was half my age and yet I found myself following him like some kind of a superhuman being.' Jhoon Rhee, the Korean karate *sensei* who first met Bruce when we moved to Los Angeles admits, 'Bruce didn't leave me with a very good image at the beginning for he was abrupt in making

19

statements. But I soon learned to give him credit for being strongminded—he really said what he believed and not many people do that; that is, unless they have something to back it up with—and Bruce certainly had that. First of all, there was his mastery of the martial arts and then there was the fact that he was a very well read person. He had thousands of books—they were all over his house [in Los Angeles] and even overflowed into the garage. I thought it amazing that such a young man had read so much—which was why when you talked to him you found his vocabulary so amazing. So that all around, he behaved like a very confident person.' Peter Chin, his friend, recalls, 'Bruce was a marvelous talker. I don't care who was there—who was in the party; even if the President of the United States had been there, Bruce would keep talking. There were a few times when he was with James Coburn and Steve McQueen—and I mean they were superstars at the time and Bruce was nothing—and yet the only voice you could hear was Bruce's. He could talk on any subject—and people just naturally listened to him.' Jim Coburn himself says, 'He was not an ordinary human being—he had this great force which he created within himself. I know a lot of people with great energy, but it's random energy—it goes out and scatters everywhere. But Bruce's incredible drive was always directed, it was always aimed towards a specific.' A Hawaiian newspaper once asked me if Bruce's real personality was much different from his screen persona and I replied, 'There was something about him that was very magnetic. He could walk into a room where there were at least ten people and after speaking only a dozen words, these people automatically found themselves being drawn to him. And then, within a minute, he would be probably entertaining the whole group. And of course it is the same magnetism, the same strength of personality which draws the screen audiences to Bruce. But the characters Bruce played were essentially different from his own personality.'

Bruce, I know, has been accused of 'needing' to be at

the center of a cult. Yet he could no more help being at the center of a cult or, indeed, anything else, than a tornado can stop twisting. He was certainly a total extrovert who loved performing—but it was all done with an almost childlike innocence; a cheerful frankness. In addition, his deep knowledge of philosophy and psychology, his wide range of reading, his wit and verbal dexterity, his easy, poised charm, his physical grace and skill, and the sheer intensity of his personality made him a natural leader. Hollywood producer Fred Weintraub insists that watching Bruce at gung fu was on a par with seeing Nijinsky dance or hearing Beethoven play the piano. When I first met Bruce, I did think him a bit cocky but I soon realized that what I was seeing was self-confidence and self-assurance, not a form of boastfulness. If Bruce said he could do something or claimed he knew something, I found he was always speaking the truth.

This, then, was the rather overpowering young man who began teaching me the elements of gung fu in a Chinatown basement. I had no idea then, of course, that I was going to fall in love with Bruce; I was only eighteen and had no intention of falling in love with anybody. Initially, I was just one of the crowd of students who gathered round him to study gung fu and generally have some fun. After lessons, we would all go on somewhere together—to a movie or out for a meal. About the same time, I became a pre-med freshman at the university itself and so began to see a lot more of him. We bumped into each other daily at the students' union building. When we were not in lectures, I was one of the group who followed him around, having fun in general and talking about gung fu. In a sense, I suppose he was a kind of guru to us all. Being around Bruce was both exhilarating and rewarding. All kinds of subjects would come up for discussion, some of them pretty serious. As James Coburn reflects about the lunch-time sessions he had with Bruce in Hollywood years later, 'We'd sit and rap ideas together—not necessarily about the martial arts but about life in general and also its

21

A young man in love,
his dreams of glory still only dreams.

esoteric values that we were both trying to get at.' But if Bruce was the opposite of superficial, he certainly was far from solemn. As Peter Chin says, 'Being around Bruce always made you feel happy. You always felt yourself laughing and feeling good. For instance, he told great jokes. Oh, sure, some of them were pretty dirty, why not?—kinda *Playboy* stuff. But a lot of them were Chinese jokes. Bruce could be funny about anything—having a pair of trousers made. And he had such a marvelous memory that he could go on telling jokes for three hours. Half the time it wasn't that the joke itself was so funny but the way Bruce dramatized it. In fact, he could repeat a joke you'd already heard—even a corny one—and make you double up. He had this gift that he could leave you still laughing and feeling happy long after he had left the room.'

When we were not taking formal lessons, we spent a great deal of our spare time practicing gung fu kicks and moves and sparring a little on a tree-secluded lawn on the campus near the academic buildings. While teaching or showing us moves he always explained the philosophy behind gung fu—what he called the Tao of Gung Fu; 'Tao' being the spontaneity of the universe, the principle underlying everything, as expressed in the Yin-Yang principle, the two mutually complementary forces at work behind all phenomena. Most of us found this very effective—we felt that we were getting more than just a boxing lesson; that we were gaining valuable insights into Oriental thinking.

Although he simply oozed self-assurance, Bruce was rarely rude or discourteous when in company; he was instinctively suave and very much the gentleman—he was certainly not like anyone else I'd met. He tended to disarm people, I think, by the sheer spontaneity of his behavior; by his good-humored informality. Of course, he possessed so much restless energy, was so wrapped up in his enthusiasms, that his behavior often seemed rather unorthodox. As his friend and lawyer Adrian Marshall puts it, 'Bruce seemed to get more out of each day than there was in it. His minutes were, well, like

23

fuller minutes. He never seemed to be goofing off—mentally and physically he didn't waste any time in any sense; I couldn't imagine Bruce at leisure.' I can confirm this. Even when watching TV, Bruce was never able to relax properly. He was constantly studying techniques. Suddenly something would spur an idea in his head and he would jump up and write it down immediately. He couldn't even read a book without doing something else at the same time. I often found him with a book in one hand and a dumbbell in the other. James Coburn recalls that during a long flight together between Delhi and Bombay, Bruce kept pounding away on a writing pad first with one hand and then the other until Jim complained, 'Hey, man, you've been doing that for an hour now—can't you stop it for a while?' Bruce apologetically explained, 'I've got to keep in shape.'

Bruce would sometimes astonish diners in a restaurant by getting up to demonstrate a movie; he was quite without inhibitions and sometimes oblivious to his surroundings, particularly when he had become immersed in a discussion. I remember that when I first knew him, he would often bring everything in the students' union cafeteria to a sudden stop. Although I have explained that Bruce was an extrovert and enjoyed giving a performance—he was unquestionably a born showman—it was not that he was deliberately trying to draw attention to himself. Someone would raise a point about the art or ask Bruce for an interpretation of one of his favorite sayings, such as 'Knowing is not enough, we must do; willing is not enough, we must apply.' And suddenly, Bruce would be on his feet, giving a practical demonstration. Within seconds, a crowd would have gathered, staring at him in fascination. It was the kind of behavior, in fact, that owed more to his sense of being a *sifu* (teacher) than to being a showman. He was obsessed by his own body's and mind's potential and wanted us to think about and get to know our own bodies and minds in the same way. Even when he had become a tremendous success, he never allowed himself to become pompous or inhibited. Fred Weintraub recalls that at a

24

time when one newspaper had already dubbed him 'The King of Hong Kong', Bruce might be seen within minutes urging complete strangers to whom he had just been introduced to 'Punch my stomach—go on!'; his sense of informality, of behaving naturally, was such that sometimes at screenings, he would strip off his shirt to be comfortable. Fred adds, 'I remember standing in line at some restaurant and Bruce would suddenly lash out a punch next to my face. I could feel the brush of air, but I was never afraid; he had absolute control, he never missed, he was like a sharpshooter.'

Jim Coburn explains, 'Bruce was constantly relating everything in life to martial arts and martial arts to everything in life—which kind of staggered me a little bit because I didn't know how to do that—how do you relate everything to martial arts? But Bruce was the personification of that . . . of the philosophical and the physical side.' He was a perfect example of how a man motivated by strong will could transform a fairly inadequate frame—after all, he was only just over five foot seven, weighed only 135 pounds, and had been as skinny as a piece of wire when a kid—into a truly lethal weapon. It was this that lay behind his demonstration of one-finger push-ups. The ability to do a one-finger push-up has nothing to do with gung fu; it simply showed to what a peak of physical condition he had brought himself. In a sense, some of the little tricks he played with people had a somewhat similar aim. Adrian Marshall tells how Bruce played 'the coin trick' on him—'Bruce put this dime in my hand and then said, "Let's see how fast you are—when I reach out for that dime, you close your fist and see if you can stop me from getting it." Well, he moved once and I closed my fist and then he moved again and once again I got my fist shut before he could grab the dime. The third time everything seemed to move a bit faster but when I closed my fist, I still had that dime tightly clutched. Or, at least, I thought I had! When I opened my fist, not only had the dime gone— there was a penny lying in my hand instead!' But, as I say, this was largely a game; a little trick.

The public demonstrations he gave of his quick reflexes were in a different category; they had more practical application to gung fu. At these demonstrations, Bruce would ask a member of the audience (generally a martial arts or karate expert) to come out on to the floor and try to block his jab. First, he would ask the man to put up his hand and he would then explain exactly what he intended to do. 'Now, I'm going to jab at your eyes'—and Bruce would then show the move in slow motion. Finally, when both were set, Bruce would produce a very quick jab. Bruce's purpose was simply to show that *nobody* could block him. Time and again I watched some of the greatest martial arts experts in America left flailing wildly as Bruce jabbed towards their faces and bodies; personally I never saw anyone block him.

One of his most spectacular gambits or moves, of course, was his one-inch punch. Anyone who has ever watched karate experts at work—or even ordinary boxing champions such as George Foreman or Muhammad Ali—may find it inconceivable that a man could deliver a paralyzingly powerful blow from a distance of one inch. The typical karate punch, in fact, originates as far back as the hip and Bruce used to say, 'Look at the time which is lost between the origination of the punch and its target. And it isn't necessary—because you can get just as much power from a shorter distance.' Eventually, it became very difficult to find anybody who would volunteer to take Bruce's one-inch punch and he used to have to bring along his own man; somebody, perhaps, like Bobby Baker, who is well over six feet tall. Bobby would stand with a punching pad protecting his chest and midriff; Bruce would stand with his right foot forward, his left a foot or so behind and his clenched fist, no more than an inch from Bobby's chest. All the spectators ever saw then was a slight lurch forward by Bruce and his left heel come up. In fact, Bruce was able to generate such power from a twist of his waist that Bobby Baker or whoever else was on the receiving end would go flying back several feet to sprawl in a waiting

26

chair—which he would hit with such impact that the chair almost tipped over. It might be said, of course, that such a punch is easy enough to fake. But Jim Coburn remembers being on the receiving end once. This happened the first time he ever met Bruce.

Jim had done quite a bit of training in karate and other martial arts for some of the films he had made. One day the writer Stirling Silliphant phoned him: 'Look, I've met a young Chinese boy who's really sensational—he's got the magic kick; he's got the magic!' So Jim and Bruce quickly got together. After they had talked for a while, Jim asked Bruce, 'Well, listen, can you show me what this *Jeet Kune Do* [Bruce's method] is?'

'Sure,' grinned Bruce. 'Stand up.'

Jim Coburn says, 'Well, I stood up—and we put a chair several feet behind me and then Bruce gave me this little one-inch punch. There isn't any adequate way to describe it. He knocked me right back—and I sprawled into the chair and the force was such that the chair actually toppled over and I rolled right into the corner area. I mean—one inch! Wow!'

I have mentioned one or two of Bruce's extraordinary qualities; but eventually I learned that living with him demanded a fair degree of patience and understanding. 'I am difficult to live with, aren't I?' he once remarked to me. He had his share of the ordinary human weaknesses. For instance, he had a very fiery temper and I think that perhaps he was very fortunate in finding himself being driven to take up gung fu as a boy for it enabled him to find a release for his frustrations and challenged his easily-sparked anger. In general, he contained his emotions and kept his anger in check. But if he was particularly frustrated, he exploded! I remember once, shortly after we were married, when we bought a king-size bed. Oddly enough, for all his skills, Bruce was not a handy man around the house; he really didn't know—or more probably didn't care to know—how to handle tools or other do-it-yourself equipment. He was never one for fixing the plumbing; if ever anything went wrong about the house, we simply called up someone. Anyway, together we tried to erect this enormous bed. Years later we were able to recall our efforts with amusement but at the time it wasn't all that funny. As soon as we put the bed together on one side, it would fall down on the other—and vice versa. I'm afraid Bruce's patience eventually snapped; he picked up this enormous box-spring mattress and hurled it with such force at the wall that he actually created a dent in the plaster. Stress and strain could, on occasions, play havoc with his creative, keyed-up temperament.

I didn't actually go out alone on a date with Bruce until October 25, 1963. He invited me to dine with him in the revolving restaurant at the top of the Space Needle (the enormous needle-like structure that was built for the Seattle World's Fair of 1962). I remember how romantic it was when he asked me out that night. We had been practicing gung fu on the grass at school. He tackled me, threw me down on the ground . . . and then asked me out! I remember that it seemed very important to me to make a good impression that evening and I actually borrowed a very fashionable dress and coat for the occasion—the Space Needle restaurant was the 'in' place to dine in Seattle. Bruce's car was a year-old Ford, specially souped up and full of gadgets—he always knew someone, either a student or a person in the car business, who would fix up his cars this way. Although he disliked wearing a suit—he hated to feel constricted —he was dressed in a well-cut Hong Kong suit and a purple shirt. He had a present for me—one of those Scandinavian troll dolls that were all the craze then. It had braided pigtails—which made me laugh, for I was taking a swimming course at the university that quarter and almost every day I walked into the students' union with my hair all wet and in pigtails.

It turned out to be a very romantic evening; everything perfect. We talked about Bruce's background and early life, which I found fascinating. We also discussed philosophy and psychology, another subject he was working on at college. What he was really excited about

28

that night, however, were his plans for a chain of gung fu schools. He had now moved the Institute to 4750 University Way, Seattle, where he had three thousand square feet of space—actually the entire ground level of an apartment house—and had managed to outfit it with a small amount of training equipment and put up a proper door sign. He was convinced by now that gung fu could provide him with his livelihood.

I was totally captivated by his magnetism and the energy which flowed from him; yet I cannot honestly say that I abruptly fell in love with Bruce that very night. I don't think most people fall genuinely in love like that. Certainly, in our case, the whole relationship was a gradual and maturing process which continued right through our whole marriage. Bruce used to say, 'Love is like a friendship caught on fire. In the beginning a flame, very pretty, often hot and fierce but still only light and flickering. As love grows older, our hearts mature and our love becomes as coals, deep-burning and unquenchable.'

After that night, certainly, falling in love became almost inevitable. I had always been a very studious girl but I found the English course at the university quite taxing and Bruce immediately came to my rescue. His mother tongue, of course, was Cantonese and when he came back to America, he had only the rudiments of English. But with typical zest and energy he sat down to learn the language thoroughly, with the result that his grammar, syntax and vocabulary became superior to those of most Americans—a command of language that was enhanced by the fact that his accent was much closer to standard English, presumably through the British influence in Hong Kong, than is usual in the United States.

Today, when I reflect on our courtship, I believe that it was our very differences in race, culture, upbringing, tradition and customs that were largely instrumental in bringing us even closer together. My family name was Emery and I suppose I was a fairly typical product of middle-American culture; as a youngster I attended

29

both Presbyterian and Baptist churches. Bruce's family were Catholic (except for his father, who was a Buddhist) and although by the time I met him he had discarded formal religion—and, indeed, could no longer be described as religious in any sense—he still remembered the *Ave Maria* and other Catholic prayers of his childhood. At least religion, therefore, was no barrier to our proposed marriage—and in the event our ethnic and cultural differences proved none either: indeed, I believe that interracial problems can exist in a marriage only if a person sets out to make them so. Bruce and I, on the contrary, found that the differences merely served to enrich us; each of us gaining new insights from the other.

My mother, who had been widowed when I was only five years old, was understandably not so optimistic. She'd had her dreams for me and had hoped to see me become a doctor one day (Bruce himself had once considered becoming a doctor). When she learned that I was seeing a Chinese-American she felt apprehensive—not because she disapproved of Bruce personally (she hardly knew him) but because she felt that our relationship might grow into something more serious and that, of course, would have shattered her ambitions for me—and besides, as she admitted to the Seattle *Times* after Bruce's death, 'I was a bit leery of a mixed marriage.' So we kind of kept it a secret that we were seeing each other alone and so far as my mother knew, I was only one of a bunch of college kids taking kung fu lessons from Bruce.

In June 1964 I realized that I faced an important decision. Bruce discovered that his Seattle Institute wasn't making anything like enough money. He attributed this, rightly I think, to the fact that Seattle is a bit of an out-of-the-way place and is rarely up on the main trend; generally catching up on things later. Besides, kung fu, karate and all the martial arts were nothing like as popular as they have since become. He realized that the right place to open a school was California which, in so many ways, is often in advance of the rest of the country.

When he had first returned to America from Hong Kong in 1959, he had stayed in Oakland, where he met the martial artist James Lee (no relation). James was considerably older than Bruce and had a very wide background in all the martial arts, but he was so intrigued by Bruce's methods and abilities that he became his first pupil—although Bruce was then only eighteen. So at the end of the term, Bruce got in touch with James again and flew down to Oakland to open a second school with James as his partner. He was so excited with the prospects for kung fu in America that he had decided to forgo graduation and put his plans into immediate action. Before leaving, he told me that if everything worked out, he would probably be staying in Oakland for some time, so we really had to make up our minds. We either had to get married—or part; possibly for good.

He came back to Seattle in early August carrying a wedding ring lent to him by James Lee's wife (in his haste, however, he forgot to pack a suit and had to rent one in which to get married). We broke the news to my mother one Friday evening and as I had foreseen she was extremely upset—particularly about the kind of problems our children might have to face. Despite her apprehensions and other understandable feelings, she bravely attended our wedding in the local Protestant church—as did my grandmother. Everything happened so quickly that I didn't even have a proper wedding dress—nor was there a photographer present.

My mother, her eyes brimming with tears, saw us off that evening for Oakland. But far from nursing any resentment towards Bruce, she soon found herself completely won over and became as convinced as I that Bruce would one day achieve everything he hoped for. She came to love and admire him very dearly and in return he called her 'Mom'. Most women, I soon discovered, found it difficult to resist Bruce's impish blandishments and my mother proved no exception—particu-

31

larly when he used to gaze at her admiringly and tell her, 'You know, mom, you've got the greatest legs of any woman of your age I've ever seen!'

THREE

Few people have started a major film career as early as Bruce did; he was scarcely three months old when he was carried on for a part in a Chinese movie made in San Francisco.

Bruce was born in San Francisco's Chinese hospital on November 27, 1940, son of Mr. and Mrs. Lee Hoi Chuen. Show business was unquestionably in his blood for his father was a famous star with the Cantonese Opera Company—a permanent company which specializes in the Chinese equivalent of music-hall or variety. In fact, the only reason Bruce was born in the United States at all was because his father happened to be on an American tour at the time. Indeed, when his mother gave birth to him, Bruce's father was three thousand miles away performing in New York's Chinatown. He was born in the year of the Dragon, in the hour of the Dragon—which is why film fans first got to know him as Lee Siu Loong, 'Little Dragon', the name given him by a film director when he became a child star. His mother Grace Lee, who was half European and a Catholic, christened him Lee Jun Fan, using the Anglicized version of Li because she realized it would be possibly mispronounced in America. The name meant 'Return to San Francisco' because, as his mother explained, she felt he would one day return and live in San Francisco. Later, the name was changed to Lee Yuen Kam when it was realized that the Chinese characters were similar to his late grandfather's. One of the nurses in the hospital gave him his English name Bruce; but it was a name never used in the family until Bruce enrolled at the La Salle College in Hong Kong many years later. At home he was always called 'Small Phoenix'—a feminine name. Mrs. Lee had lost her first son and according to Chinese tradition when future sons are born in a family, they are usually addressed by a girl's name in order to confuse the spirits who might steal away their souls. He also had one ear pierced to distract the gods.

His parents returned to Hong Kong when Bruce was still only three months old, to their large flat (by Hong Kong standards) at 218 Nathan Road, Kowloon. The change of climate had a disastrous effect on the child and Bruce almost didn't make it; for a long time he was very sickly. When I reflect on Bruce's life and career they always seem to me to contain the sheer stuff of melodrama; so much about him smacks of the incredible. I know that millions of his fans are convinced that Bruce was born with a special body; they have watched him exercise his extraordinary strength; seen his agility; studied him as he flexed his small but marvelously-muscled frame. Many of them simply do not believe it when I explain that Bruce built up his outstanding physique through sheer application and will-power; through intense training. As a child, he never ate much and for a long time remained thin and, apparently, delicate.

Conditions in Chinese homes in Hong Kong are often fairly primitive but the Lee family never really lacked for anything—except, perhaps, space. At that time, in early 1941, Mr. Lee's family consisted of himself, Grace, Phoebe, Agnes, Peter and Bruce. Mrs. Lee's first child, a son, had died in infancy and—again according to Chinese tradition—it is believed that if there is to be good luck, the second child must be a girl; fortunately they had Phoebe. It is easy to dismiss these old superstitions but one sometimes is made to pause and wonder. A Chinese fortune-teller had told Mr. Lee when he was a young man that he would die before his sixty-fourth birthday. He had at least one narrow escape from death

33

—when, during the Japanese attack on Hong Kong in December 1941, a bomb crashed through the roof of the bulding where Mr. Lee, a licensed opium smoker and a friend were having a pipe and although the bomb failed to explode, it crashed onto the bed next to Mr. Lee's and plunged down into the basement carrying the body of his friend with it. In 1965 his health was deteriorating and he died shortly after his 64th birthday.

Sharing the flat, too, however, were Mr. Lee's sister-in-law and her five children. On the death of his brother, Mr. Lee, as is the Chinese custom, had taken the whole family into his own home and supported them as he would his own family. Together with a couple of other relatives, some Cantonese servants and a young boy whom Mr. Lee had adopted and who remained Bruce's close friend and helper throughout his life, this meant that more than sixteen people were crowded into the flat. Add to that Mr. Lee's dogs, birds and fish—he had nine dogs, seven birds and many fish—and it may be easier to understand why Bruce was able to roam the streets unsupervised to such an extent. Why he became, in his own words, 'a bit of a punk'.

Bruce had his favorite among the dogs. Bobby was an Alsatian and he and Bruce more or less adopted each other. Bobby used to sleep under Bruce's bed and, in the days before Bruce became a martial artist, often protected him when another street urchin attempted to hit him. When Bobby died, Bruce wept and was almost inconsolable.

It is perhaps ironic in view of his eventual tremendous success that initially Bruce threatened to become the black sheep of the family (his older brother, Peter, is now a distinguished and respected scientist with the Royal Observatory in Hong Kong). From the beginning, he was the nonconformist; the one who was different. There was a wild, dynamic, joyous streak about him deriving from his tremendous energy and theatrical flair. Nothing except books could keep Bruce quiet or still for more than a second. He was simply bouncing with energy—running, talking, jumping up and down, playing tricks; he grabbed at life as though it were a big rosy apple. Give him an absorbing book, however, and he would sit and read for hours, lost in another world. His mother doted on him and it was largely due to her that he did not end up a juvenile delinquent. He was close to his father, whom he both feared and respected. It was through his father's connections that Bruce became a child film star. His father used to bring him backstage at the theaters and took him on tours during school vacations; Bruce also hung around the set when his father was appearing in a film (oddly enough, they never appeared together). It was largely from his father that Bruce appears to have derived much of his temperament and, most certainly, his acting ability. His father was a comedian and had a very dynamic presence on stage.

Bruce usually discounted his appearance on film at the age of three months and dated his real screen career from his role in *The Beginning of a Boy*, which he made in Hong Kong when he was six. He was eight when he played his second role—under the name Lee Siu Loong, or 'Little Dragon', the name by which he became best known in Hong Kong and on the Mandarin film circuit of Southeast Asia. All told, he made twenty films before he was eighteen, the last of them a starring role in *The Orphan* which was released shortly before he left Hong Kong for America. He worked mainly at night and his mother recalls, 'He liked it very much. At two o'clock in the morning, I'd call out "Bruce, the car is here," and he'd leap up and put his shoes on and go off very cheerfully. There was no trouble at all getting him up when it came to making a film. When I had to get him up for school in the mornings, however, it was different.'

Bruce's boyhood has now become legendary. The true picture that emerges, I think, is of a boy who learned the hard way how to take care of himself. People brought up in such cities as Seattle, as I was really have little conception of life as it is lived, particularly by the Chinese, in the teeming colony of Hong Kong. The

35

island of Hong Kong, with the city of Victoria and its suburbs in the New Territories (that part of the Chinese mainland held by the British under lease) is, in the main a cramped, crowded, exciting, jostling place. Nor ought it to be forgotten, either, that it is a place where people have had to struggle fiercely to survive. Bruce spent his childhood there during the savage Japanese occupation —he once perched himself perilously astride the wall of the veranda two stories above Nathan Road to shake his fist at a Japanese plane flying overhead—and lived there during the tumultuous and dangerous years that followed the Communist triumph in mainland China when a constant stream of refugees, many fleeing famine conditions, poured into the colony.

Gangs of young Chinese boys roamed the streets of Kowloon, seeking adventure and amusement and distraction wherever they could find it. In essence, their behavior was not all that much different from the kind of gang 'rumbles' then taking place in cities like New York, Chicago, and Los Angeles. Bruce, with his excessive energy and fighting instincts—for Bruce was a fighter first and foremost and everything else afterwards —was soon in there with the toughest; he was a born competitor. Torn out of context, his behavior can be made to seem worse than it really was. He told *Black Belt* magazine in October 1967, 'I was a punk and went looking for fights. We used chains and pens with knives hidden inside them.' His family remembers that Bruce kept these 'weapons' in a wardrobe. Bruce usually wore a toilet chain wrapped around his waist when he went out on the streets and told his younger brother Robert, 'it's handy when you get into a fight'. On the whole, the 'weapons' were more for bravado than anything else; Bruce believed in using his fists. His brothers recall that, if Bruce didn't like someone, he told him straight to his face—which meant he found plenty of trouble. At school he was anything but an avid student; history or social subjects interested him but he detested maths and his mother says that by the time he was ten, that was as far as he could count. His bad school record and gen-

36

eral behavior led to his being asked to leave a few of the Chinese schools. He was about twelve or thirteen when he was admitted to La Salle College. At this period, his father was very disturbed at the way Bruce was conducting himself and neglecting his studies. While he was compassionate and understanding enough about his fighting—the boy had to work off his excess energy in some way in a teeming area of four-and-a-half-million people—he thought his film-making was a greater hindrance to his studies and Mr. Lee made one or two attempts to intervene. But the Hong Kong directors and producers liked Bruce so much, that they dissuaded his father.

Shortly after he entered La Salle College (we sent Brandon to the same school years later) Bruce came home one day and told his mother that he wanted to be trained in the martial arts. He said that he was being bullied at school and wanted to learn how to defend himself properly. His father, of course, practiced Tai Chi Chuan, which is a series of exercises and moves carried out in slow motion. Any morning all over Hong Kong or in mainland China itself you can see millions of men going through the motions of Tai Chi Chuan. Bruce had joined his father once or twice doing Ti Chi Chuan but although it is also a form of self-defense, its purpose is mainly therapeutic—and what Bruce had in mind had nothing to do with therapy. His mother was sympathetic and agreed to pay the twelve Hong Kong dollars per lesson. His teacher was the great master, Yip Man, an expert in Wing Chun. This style had been originally developed by a monastery nun called Yin Wing Chun ('Beautiful springtime') about three hundred or four hundred years ago; a style of defense ideally suited to women or other persons unable to exercise simple brute force.

To me, looking back on my husband's life, perhaps one of the most interesting aspects of all is the way he grew, matured and blossomed in so many different ways—physically and mentally. The truly remarkable essence of Bruce's life is not the skills he achieved, nor the money he made, nor the fame he created, great as all these were and are. The great achievement is what he made of himself. Physically, he turned a skinny, delicate frame into a marvelous tool; mentally, I believe, he made even greater strides.

To illustrate what I mean, it might perhaps be worth reproducing an essay Bruce wrote for his English course as a freshman at the university. He called it 'A Moment of Understanding': 'Gung Fu is a special kind of skill; a fine art rather than just a physical exercise. It is a subtle art of matching the essence of the mind to that of the technique in which it has to work. The principle of Gung Fu is not a thing that can be learned, like a science, by fact finding and instruction in facts. It has to grow spontaneously, like a flower, in a mind free from emotion and desires. The core of this principle of Gung Fu is *Tao*—the spontaneity of the universe.

'After four years of hard training in the art of Gung Fu, I began to understand and felt the principle of gentleness—the art of neutralizing the effect of the opponent's effort and minimizing expenditure of one's energy. All these must be done in calmness and without striving. It sounded simple, but in actual application it was difficult. The moment I engaged in combat with an opponent, my mind was completely perturbed and unstabled. Especially after a series of exchanging blows and kicks, all my theory of gentleness was gone. My only one thought left was somehow or another I must beat him and win.

'My instructor Professor Yip head of Win Chun School, would come up to me and say, "Loong, relax and calm your mind. Forget about yourself and follow the opponent's movement. Let your mind, the basic reality, to do the counter-movement without any interfering deliberation. Above all, learn the art of detachment."

'That was it! I must relax. However, right there I had already done something contradictory, against my will. That was when I said I must relax, the demand for effort in "must" was already inconsistent with the effortlessness in "relax". When my acute self-consciousness grew to what the psychologists called "double-blind" type, my instructor would again approach me and say, "Loong, preserve yourself by following the natural bends of things and don't interfere. Remember never to assert yourself against nature: never be in frontal opposition to any problems, but to control it by swinging with it. Don't practice this week. Go home and think about it."

'The following week I stayed home. After spending many hours in meditation and practice, I gave up and went sailing alone in a junk. On the sea I thought of all my past training and got mad at myself and punched at the water. Right then at that moment, a thought suddenly struck me. Wasn't this water, the very basic stuff, the esssence of Gung Fu? Didn't the common water just illustrated to me the principle of Gung Fu? I struck it just now, but it did not suffer hurt. Again I stabbed it with all my might, yet it was not wounded. I then tried to grasp a handful of it but it was impossible. This water, the softest substance in the world, could fit itself into any container. Although it seemed weak, it could penetrate the hardest substance in the world. That was it! I wanted to be like the nature of water.

'Suddenly a bird flew past and cast its reflection on the water. Right then, as I was absorbing myself, another mystic sense of hidden meaning started upon me. Shouldn't it be the same then that the thoughts and emotions I had in front of an opponent passed like the reflection of the bird over the water? This was exactly what Professor Yip meant by being detached—not being without emotion or feeling, but being one in whom feeling was not sticky or blocked. Therefore in order to control myself I must first accept myself by going with, and not against, my nature.

'I lay on the boat and felt that I had united with Tao; I had become one with nature. I just lay there and let the boat drift freely and irresistibly according to its own will. For at that moment I have achieved a state of inner feeling in which opposition had become mutually cooperative instead of mutually exclusive, in which there was

Bruce demonstrating his famous one-inch punch.

no longer any conflict in my mind. The whole world to me was unitary.'

This was the way Bruce's mind was to work at age eighteen or twenty. But he had all this to learn and discover when he first began studying with Yip Man. He was still a tough, wild, rebellious little kid, armed with a chain, a knife and a pair of knuckledusters, generally out in front of a little band, full of eagerness and fighting spirit. Fights would start over little or nothing. Dares were the common catalyst. Bruce would run into another youngster in the street and the two would 'stare' at each other— challenging with their eyes. Nobody ever knew Bruce to back down from a 'stare'—he used to tell his brothers and other relatives that nobody had ever 'out-stared' him. And his brother Robert remembers that, as soon as a couple of kids anywhere began scrapping, of course, the whole thing quickly deteriorated into a gang-fight.

Bruce has been portrayed as a juvenile rebel and potential delinquent but, by and large, I believe this to be an exaggerated picture. Bruce, I'm convinced, was basically much too intelligent, had too many of the perceptions of an artist not to have realized eventually where to draw the line himself. Many of his escapades were no more than might be expected from any high-spirited, spunky young fighter. All the kids attending the La Salle College were Chinese Catholics and there was intense rivalry between them and the British schoolchildren attending the King George V School up the hill. The Hong Kong Chinese are not all that fond of the British; an understandable attitude in view of the history of the place and the relationship based on illusions of superiority and inferiority between the races. After school, Bruce and a crowd of his fellow Chinese students would gather on the hill to taunt the English boys. Some fierce encounters followed and it was in these kinds of battles that Bruce first learned how to apply the principles of classical kung fu to the realities of dealing with opponents who were blissfully unaware of the correct forms and whose reactions and behavior were totally unpredictable—the basis of his own 'method' (which he would prefer to call teaching) and which he called Jeet Kune Do, the Way of the Intercepting Fist, described by him 'as a sophisticated form of (street) fighting'.

Bruce flung himself into the study of kung fu with frenetic energy; once his interest was aroused in anything, he became a kind of primeval force; his appetite to learn and conquer was quite voracious. His devotion to kung fu was total. While other students might skip classes, Bruce attended *every* day immediately after school. One trick he employed to get more personal tuition from Yip Man himself was to stand on the stairs before class was due to commence and tell the other students as they arrived 'No class today'—leaving himself the sole recipient of the old man's wisdom and attention for that session. The intensity of Bruce's obsession surprised his fellows. He seemed to *live* kung fu. One moment he would be deeply immersed in thought, the next jumping around and hitting out as he attempted to put into practice the ideas that had been racing through his head. Walking in the street, he would surprise passersby by throwing punches and moving his body (the spectacular kicks which later became familiar to movie-goers were *no* part of the Wing Chun style). At home, he could not sit through a meal without pounding away with alternate hands on a stool beside him, to toughen his hands and strengthen his muscles. Two months after he took up kung fu, he was able to again challenge a boy who had earlier defeated him, and this time it was Bruce who got the better of him. 'I've been learning Wing Chun,' grinned Bruce. In fact, it was more a matter of confidence than expertise, for none of the martial arts can transform a fighter so quickly.

By the time he was fifteen, Bruce was a considerable figure among the kids living in his neighborhood of Kowloon. He was extremely good-looking—and knew it. He was at that age when a boy begins to take an interest in the opposite sex. His brother Peter recalls that Bruce would spend up to fifteen minutes in front of the mirror, getting his hair just right, making sure his tie was properly adjusted and so on. There was an element of narcissism involved in this, of course, normal to most young people. Certainly, his looks and self-confidence, together with his reputation as a battler, meant that he had no difficulty attracting feminine attention. His attitude towards girls was nicely-balanced, too—just the right mixture of self-assurance, sensitivity and easy grace. In short, he brought a formidable battery of charms to bear on females who came within his orbit, for on top of everything else, he proved to be an outstanding dancer. In 1958 Bruce won the Crown Colony cha-cha championship. It has been reported that he had special cards made with a message asking a girl to smile if she were prepared to jump into the sack with him, which cards he handed out from time to time—but this was never more than a joke. Somebody, in fact, gave him one card and he showed it around once or twice. It was all an amusing little trick, for few girls were unable to keep themselves from smiling or laughing when the card was presented.

He was constantly in scrapes. When we visited La Salle College to see about Brandon's enrollment, the headmaster, Brother Henry, had a clear recollection of Bruce's own student days there. He told me about an occasion when the faculty were meeting in a part of the school normally out of bounds to students—indeed, it was regarded as almost sacrilegious for a boy to set foot in that area—when the door suddenly burst open and in came Bruce, racing like mad. He ran around the table once or twice where the reverend brothers sat frozen in their seats, mouths agape. Then he dived into a phone booth and squatted down out of sight. Brother Henry, having recovered his wits, asked Bruce to explain his extraordinary behavior. Bruce spun him a yarn about some boys chasing him with the intention of beating him up. This was partly true—but was hardly the whole truth, for Bruce neglected to tell Brother Henry that it was he, Bruce, who had started the trouble. He had picked a fight with another boy—and soon had a whole mob baying for his blood. Brother Henry smiled at his recollection of the lengths to which Bruce was prepared to go, even at that early age, to outwit his enemies.

Bruce has been accused of being a bit of a bully in his schooldays; certainly, he was determined to take charge and be a dominant figure. By the time he was 'asked' to leave La Salle College (he moved on to St. Francis Xavier) he was, according to his younger brother Robert, 'recognized as the king gorilla—boss of the whole school'. It was not so much that Bruce stalked around inflicting physical punishment on less able kids as that he never backed down from a challenge and, having established an outstanding reputation as a gutsy fighter and kung fu expert, had reached a position where most of the other kids recognized him as 'the one to avoid'. As Robert puts it, 'you didn't have to ask Bruce twice to fight'. When I look at old pictures of my husband, taken when he was at St. Francis Xavier, I often find it hard to believe that he was a wild kid. The group class pictures show him extremely neat and well dressed in his school blazer, his hair tidily arranged—and, in his glasses, looking every inch the serious student. He looked anything but a rebel; instead, much more the studious young man who inscribed the following earnest entries in his diary for 1958 (note how poor his English was then):

November 30, 1958: 'Now I try to find out my career —wether as a doctor or another? If as a doctor I must study hard.'
Dec 1, 1958: 'learn more mathematics.
learn more English (conversation)'.

To get a more rounded picture, however, it is perhaps necessary also to read two entries for earlier that year:

March 29, 1958: 'win the inter-school competition (champion) against 3 years champ Garie Elm. Place: St. Georgie School'.
May 2, 1958: 'against Chinese boxer student of Lung Chi Chuen (4 years training). Results: won (that guy got fainted, one tooth got out, but I got a black eye)
Place: Union Road (Kowloon City).'

The first two entries reflect the fact that Bruce did not like school and was not doing well in his studies. His mathematics were deplorable—he never got beyond the stage of simple addition and subtraction—and he managed to stay in school at all only because he bullied other youngsters into doing his homework for him. In the end, in fact, he never had any hope of graduating from secondary school and, had he stayed on in Hong Kong, he would never have got to college (Bruce did a complete 360-degree turnabout when he arrived in the United States in late 1958, buckling down to his studies and graduating from Edison High Technical School in Seattle with good enough marks to be admitted to the

University of Washington; a revolution encompassing more than just his studies).

The entries referring to his gladiatorial exploits mark the climax of Bruce's career as a potential delinquent; a wild, youthful, hedonistic phase when he sought desperately and probably unconsciously to assert himself and his personality against the world; to emerge from the teeming millions as a man with a specific identity and possessed of specific gifts. To be a film star with a face known to millions before he was eighteen was hardly the best preparation for building a stable personality; when one adds to this the physical and mental dominance he had established over his contemporaries with his fighting and other skills, I think it remarkable that Bruce managed to come to America as such a well-balanced and essentially likeable, even admirable personality.

Shortly after joining Yip Man's school, Bruce found himself tagging along in the wake of two older boys, Wong Suen-leung and Cheung Cheuk-hing, also pupils of the Wing Chun master who, having learned the rudiments of the style, were keen to challenge boxers of the other schools of kung fu (there are at least one hundred fifty different 'styles' or 'forms' of Chinese boxing). In the main, these were pretty well-conducted and sportsmanlike encounters—young men testing their courage, strength, skills and energies against each other. The two 'big brothers' plus Bruce, 'the little brother' formed the backbone of the Wing Chun challengers. To start with, the tests were limited to a handful of participants on either side and were always staged in secret. Eventually, the battles became bigger and more open with rival groups hiring cars and driving out into open spaces in the New Territories. Here judges were selected, rules laid down and a 'ring' prepared. These 'matches' continued for a number of years with Bruce and other Wing Chun specialists invariably—but not always—coming out on the winning side. Yip Chun, son of Yip Man, recalls that Bruce at this time was

45

'boxing crazy'—putting everything he had into the martial arts.

Once, when Yip Chun and Bruce were out walking together, Yip suddenly discovered that Bruce was missing. Retracing his steps, he found Bruce sitting at the side of the road, deep in thought. Then he got to his feet and began shooting out punches in all directions.

The third diary entry arose directly out of the great interest taken in Bruce by an Irish brother at St. Francis Xavier. Brother Kenny had sparred once or twice with Bruce and, realizing just how good he was, encouraged him to enter the inter-school boxing championships— boxing, that is, under the Marquess of Queensberry rules. In later years, Bruce was to find himself often involved in discussions about how well he might acquit himself against a champion such as Muhammad Ali. It is almost impossible to judge how a man practicing one style of combat might acquit himself against another with an entirely different style; possibly a champion wrestler, for instance, would always beat a champion boxer. Certainly, the great John L. Sullivan, when champion of the world, took a terrible hammering from a practitioner of *le savate,* the French version of kung fu which, like kung fu itself, probably derives from the ancient Greek *pankration* brought to India by Alexander the Great and which spread from there to Mongolia and China.

In the inter-schools final. Bruce met an English boy from King George V school who had been champion for three years in succession. Bruce adopted his kung fu stance and waited for the other boy, who commenced dancing around in the approved fashion, to attack. As soon as he did so, Bruce knocked him out—in the first round.

Trouble, however, was just over the horizon for Bruce. According to Robert, a challenge was issued to the young men of the Wing Chun school by students of the Choy Lay Fut. On May 2, the two groups met on the roof of an apartment block in the Resettlement area (that part of Kowloon housing refugees from mainland

46

China). Many of these rooftops are laid out as basketball courts and the rule was that whichever school was first to force its opponents over a white line won the contest. The encounter, of course, was not meant to be violent; merely a series of sparring engagements. It began in friendly fashion but turned ugly when a Choy Lay Fut man gave Bruce a black eye. Robert insists, 'Bruce wasn't prepared—it was only supposed to be sparring—and became really upset. That drove Bruce into a fight situation. He gave a series of straight punches [the Wing Chun style rarely employs kicks]. Bruce was powerfully fast and the guy couldn't take it—he was driven back. Bruce got him in the face several times and he fell back over the line. Bruce, still in a temper, lashed out with a couple of kicks, catching the guy in the eye and in the mouth and knocking out a tooth or two.'

The victim's parents complained to the police and Mrs. Lee had to go down to the local police station and sign a paper saying that she would take responsibility for Bruce's future good conduct if released in her care. She then took Bruce to a nearby café and had a quiet discussion with him about his future. She warned him that if his father ever head about the incident he would be extremely upset—and Bruce, who feared his father, was suitably chastened. Mrs. Lee said nothing about the affair to the other members of the family but shortly afterwards suggested to her husband that Bruce, now eighteen, should exercise his rights and opt for American citizenship. 'He hasn't any heart in his studies,' she explained to Mr. Lee.

Before he left for San Francisco aboard a steamship and with only one hundred American dollars in his pocket, Mrs. Lee warned Bruce that unless he made something of himself, he was not to come back. Bruce promised to behave himself and only return 'when I've made some money'.

The next time she saw him, Mrs. Lee had every reason to be proud of her cheeky, rebellious son. He had worked hard and was beginning to make a name for himself in America. He returned the prodigal son, a success.

FOUR

For Bruce, America at first proved no tougher nor easier than it had been for millions of immigrants before him. Indeed, on his arrival he was better equipped than most; to begin with, he was a citizen and he had at least a rudimentary grasp of English, although he had to work hard to improve it.

He could find shelter and work of a kind, too, among the various Chinese communities already there. He first stayed with an old friend of his father's in San Francisco and earned a few small sums giving dancing lessons. Then Ruby Chow, a Seattle restaurant owner and important figure in local politics, offered him a room above her restaurant in return for his services as a waiter and as a gesture of friendship to his father. Bruce jumped at the chance of a steady job and moved to Seattle. He followed the classic American pattern of studying hard by day and working hard by night to get to college. He enrolled in Edison Technical High School and at night worked in Ruby Chow's, often doubling with a job as a newspaper 'stuffer' or 'inserter' (inserting loose advertisements or give-away announcements inside the printed pages) on the Seattle *Times*. Eventually, he set up a pad in the corner of Ruby Chow's kitchen where he practiced his kung fu while waiting for customers.

By this time Bruce was determined to succeed. As he was to write some fourteen years later: 'Ever since I was a kid I have had this instinctive urge for expansion and growth. To me, the function and duty of a human being, a "quality" human being, that is, is the sincere and honest development of potential and self-actualization. Though I have to interrupt here to say that at one time, quite a long time ago, I did get a kick out of "self-image actualization" rather than "self-actualization". I have come to discover through earnest personal experience and dedicated learning that ultimately the greatest help is self-help; that there is no other help but self-help—doing one's best, dedicating one's self wholeheartedly to a given task, which happens to have no end but is an on-going process. I have done a lot during these years of my process. Well, in my process, I have changed from self-image actualization to self-actualization, from blindly following propaganda, organized truths etc. to search internally for the cause of my ignorance.'

At Edison, Bruce began in earnest that long battle to understand himself and his art which, as he himself says, 'happens to have no end'. He forced himself to work hard at math and science, the areas in which he was most ignorant, although managing to enjoy himself in history and philosophy. In gaining his high school diploma, he secured good all-around marks which admitted him to the University of Washington—something which his family would have considered an impossible or unlikely feat only two years earlier. He was a determined and dynamic young man, confident of his own abilities and, like all outstanding personalities who are not prepared to follow the crowd, clashed frequently with other strong personalities while at the same time attracting his own devoted friends and followers. Among the latter was a Japanese-American called Taky Kimura, then thirty-three. By this time, Bruce was beginning to become known to a small coterie interested in the martial arts. He had demonstrated in places as far apart as San Francisco, Los Angeles and Vancouver, where he had made a stunning impact and had already started impromptu teaching in Seattle.

'I was taking judo about 1959', explains Taky, who had been interned during the Second World War and as a consequence of this and difficulties in finding a job in the post-war world during the prevailing anti-Nipponese climate, and had lost a great deal of self-confidence and had taken to the martial arts in the hope of restoring some of it. 'I got hurt two or three times by some people who offered me nothing but brawn. I was really getting demoralized by that time. Some of the people who went to one of Bruce's classes, came by the supermarket where I was working. They told me how they met this amazing young man from Hong Kong. Of course, I thought to myself, well, I've seen a little bit of everything and it can't be that much. But they kept on telling me that he was "incredible". At that time, these fellas were practicing out in the back yards and in city parks. So I went out to the university area, to the football field and that's when I first met him. I was so amazed and impressed with his ability that I immediately asked him if I could join his club and for almost a year we just met at parks on Sundays. I was intrigued by his tremendous power, of being light one minute and really deep the next.'

As his friend Jhoon Rhee has said, Bruce generally tended to be direct and straightforward in his remarks, particularly when talking about the martial arts. In his almost desperate attempts to explain himself and his ideas without ambiguity, he often found himself clashing with exponents of classical kung fu, karate and other forms. Later, in 1967, he summed up his ideas tersely but unequivocally to *Black Belt* magazine. He insisted that kung fu had to rest on 'realism and plausibility' and argued that it was difficult to find worthwhile instruction in the art: 'There's too much horsing around with unrealistic stances and classic forms and rituals,' he explained. 'It's just too artificial and mechanical and doesn't really prepare a student for actual combat. A guy could get clobbered while getting into his classical mess. Classical methods like these, which I consider a form of paralysis, only solidify and condition what was once fluid. Their practitioners are merely blindly rehearsing systematic routines and stunts that will lead to

50

nowhere.' He described this type of teaching as little more than 'organized despair', and, commenting on classical versions of kung fu, emphasized the virtues of simplicity and directness. 'To me, a lot of this fancy stuff is not functional,' he told the interviewer.

A Japanese karate black belt attending one of Bruce's early demonstrations objected to opinions and ideas expressed along similar lines and challenged Bruce. Bruce tried to explain that he intended nothing personal and that he was not attempting to downgrade anyone else but merely explaining the essence of his own methods. The karate expert repeated his challenge and Bruce was forced to accept. The two repaired to a nearby gym, followed by a large, excited crowd. The fight was short and spectacular. The karate man opened up with a kick which Bruce, still using the Wing Chun method, blocked. Using his straight punches, typical of Wing Chun, Bruce drove the belt back towards the white line and then knocked him across it, finishing off with a kick to the eye; total time—eleven seconds. The karate expert was so impressed that he became one of Bruce's closest friends and admirers. As Bob Wall, the West Coast karate *sensei* once said, 'The one thing I hate about Bruce is he can do anything he says.' To which Taky Kimura added, 'A lot of people took exception, but when they saw what he could do, they all wanted to join him.'

As Bruce explained to his students at the time, however, it was far from being as simple as all that. He insisted, 'Mere technical knowledge of Gung Fu is not enough to make a man really its master; he ought to have delved deeply into the inner spirit of it. The spirit is grasped only when his mind is in complete harmony with the principle of life itself, that is, when he attains to a certain state in Taoism known as 'no-mindedness'. 'No-mindedness' consists in preserving the absolute fluidity of the mind by keeping it free from intellectual deliberations and affective disturbances of any kind at all. I believe that everybody can think himself into his goal if he mixes his thoughts with definitions of purpose,

51

persistence, and a burning desire for its translation into reality.' He tended to teach through a series of aphorisms—many of which not only express his philosophy of how to fight but which he attempted to put into practice in his everyday life:

> Not being tense but ready
> Not thinking but not dreaming
> Not being set but flexible
> Liberation from the uneasy sense of confinement
> It is being wholly and quietly alive, aware and alert,
> ready for whatever may come.

Initially, he had been sorely tempted, shortly after his arrival in San Francisco, to open a *kwoon* and go into teaching right away. He told *Black Belt* that several karatemen he had met during his first six months there 'wanted me to start a dojo (kwoon) in San Francisco but I wasn't interested. I wanted to further my education.' He also recalled that he disliked the odd jobs he had to do to support himself when he first came to Seattle and added, half-jokingly, 'I was too lazy for that and began teaching gung fu on the side.' In fact, he could no more abandon kung fu, even temporarily, than he could stop breathing—and besides, as a *sifu,* he earned more. As for being lazy . . . !

Margaret Walters, formerly professor at the university, recalls, in fact, that Bruce was a very dynamic young man'. She remembers: 'My whole association with him was rather amusing. I taught Freshman English and Bruce showed up. I can't remember if he got into my class through the regular hazards of registration or whether he talked his way into my class on the grounds that he had heard that I was a reasonably good teacher. It was probably the last because the classes were limited to so many students—like twenty-five—and once the class was full, you're not supposed to let other people in. But once in a while, you get a student that talks his way in and just insists and you put him in the class . . . what the registrar doesn't know, doesn't hurt too much.

He spoke good English at the time but writing themes of the kind that teachers assign are not easy for students who come from another background. It just doesn't click with them. And so I more or less let Bruce write what he wanted that first quarter. He was quite homesick, so I got these descriptions of Hong Kong. I'm pretty sure that some of the things he gave me as themes must have been translations of Chinese poetry that he had studied or read or memorized in the past. And in fact I accused him once of doing that and he sort of laughed. He didn't admit it, but he didn't deny it, either.

'In the second quarter, he launched out into a very ambitious piece of writing which was actually an explanation of the Tao philosophy. As you know, his work in kung fu was very closely related to his spiritual ideas. So he wrote this almost book-length thing about the whole philosophy of Lao-tzu, the founder. That was very interesting. I must say that I learned a lot from it.'

Bruce, in fact, wrote *two* long dissertations on the philosophical principles underpinning kung fu (perhaps I ought to explain again that, in Cantonese, the word is pronounced Gung fu; when the Chinese pictographs are translated into the Roman alphabet, the word appears as kung fu but the only time the letter K is pronounced as K and not as G is when it is succeeded by an apostrophe). I believe it is almost impossible to understand Bruce and what his life was about without delving, however briefly, into these two papers which he wrote as part of his philosophy course. The first, which he partly illustrated (among his other talents Bruce could draw and paint), he entitled:

THE ART OF GUNG FU

Gung Fu (Chinese art of pugilism), the oldest of all hand to hand combat, is practiced for health promotion, cultivation of mind, and self-protection. Because it has been shrouded under a veil of utmost secrecy, Gung Fu is almost unknown to the outside world.

Its history covers five thousand years. At first, in the mists of antiquity, Gung Fu was simply no-hold-barred

Bruce demonstrating one of the kicks he made famous the world over.

fighting, but as the centuries went by, countless generations of its practitioners gradually perfected it, smoothing out the rough spots, polishing the techniques, until it began to emerge as something definitely superior. Since, to a great extent, Gung Fu was used by Chinese monks and Taoist priests, they also saw, and taught, the connection between the mental and the physical aspects. Gung Fu to them, and to any serious student of the art, is more than just an excellent fighting system; simply using it to kill or maim an opponent is not its purpose. Gung Fu is a philosophy, is an integral part of the philosophies of Taoism and Buddhism, the ideals of giving with adversity, to bend slightly and then spring up stronger than before, to have patience in all things, to profit by one's mistakes and lessons in life. These are the many-sided aspects of the art of Gung Fu, it teaches the way to live, as well as the way to protect oneself. There are two main schools in Gung Fu; the 'hard' and the 'soft' school. The hard school concentrates on speed, coordination of movements, and physical power, which is like cracking bricks and stones with bare hands; or, with blinding speed, to disable several attackers in a matter of seconds. This school concentrates mostly on the 'outside,' so to speak; on firmness and substantiality, and more on aggressiveness. The soft school, on the other hand, concentrates and believes in gentleness, and unity of mind and body, in which firmness is trained in harmony with the breath, which in turn exercises the body. This school concentrates mostly on the 'inside', so to speak; on softness and insubstantiality. However, both of these two schools possess some degree of firmness and softness, substantiality and insubstantiality.

From these two schools of Gung Fu branched off hundreds of different clans, each having a method of its own. Here I'll just mention some of the names of the different clans:—The 'Eagle Claw' clan, which is famous for its powerful development of the hand; the 'Mantis' clan is noted for its strong forearm and kicking technique; the 'Tai Kik' is famous for its gentleness; the 'Choy Li Fat' is noted for its power and its long-range type of fighting; the 'Buat Kwa', its gentleness and footwork; the 'White Crane', its blinding technique, etc.'

Bruce's study of philosophy embraced the teachings of Buddha, Confucius, Lao-tzu, the founders of Taoism and other Oriental thinkers and spiritual leaders. The rest of the paper is given up to a distillation of the wisdom of such teachers. The foundation of everything is the Yin-Yang principle, generally represented by the Double Fish symbol (which Bruce used as the insignia of his various clubs and which he also had inscribed on his personal business cards).

In his second paper, entitled "The Tao of Gung Fu." Bruce wrote:

> 'To the Chinese, Gung Fu is a subtle art of match-
> ing the essence of the mind to that of the techniques
> in which it has to work. The principle of Gung Fu is
> not a thing that can be learned, like a science, by
> fact-finding and instruction in facts. It has to grow
> spontaneously, like a flower, in a mind free from emo-
> tions and desires. The core of this principle of Gung
> Fu is "Tao"—the spontaneity of the universe.'

He explains that the word has no exact equivalent in English, but suggests using the word 'Truth'—and proceeds to explain the 'Truth' that every Gung Fu practitioner should follow:

> 'Tao operates in Yin and Yang, a pair of mutually
> complementary forces that are at work in and behind
> all phenomena. This principle of Yin-Yang, also
> known as Tai Chi, is the basic structure of Gung Fu.
> The Tai Chi or Grand Terminus was first drawn more
> than three thousand years ago, by Chou Chun. The
> Yang (whiteness) principle represents positiveness,
> firmness, maleness, substantiality, brightness, day, heat,
> etc. The Yin (blackness) principle is the opposite. It
> represents negativeness, softness, femaleness, insub-
> stantiality, darkness, night, coldness and so forth.
> The basic theory in Tai Chi is that nothing is so

permanent as never to change. In other words, when activity reaches the extreme point, it becomes inactivity, and inactivity forms Yin. Extreme inactivity returns to become activity, which is Yang. Activity is the cause of inactivity, and vice-versa. This system of complementary increasing and decreasing of the principle is continuous. From this one can see that the two forces, although they appear to conflict, in reality are mutually interdependent; instead of opposition, there is cooperation and alternation.

The application of the Principles of Yin and Yang in Gung Fu are expressed as the Law of Harmony. It states that one should be in harmony with, not rebellion against, the strength and force of the opposition. This means that one should do nothing that is not natural or spontaneous; the important thing is not to strain in any way. When opponent A uses strength (Yang) on B, B must not resist him (back) with strength; in other words, do not use positiveness (Yang) against positiveness (Yang) but instead yield to him with softness (Yin) and lead him to the direction of his own force, negativeness (Yin) to positiveness (Yang). When A's strength goes to the extreme, the positiveness (Yang) will change to negativeness (Yin), B then taking him at his unguarded moment and attacking with force (Yang). Thus the whole process is without being unnatural or strained. B fits his movement harmoniously and continuously into that of A without resisting or striving.

The above idea gives rise to a closely related Law, the Law of Noninterference with nature, which teaches a Gung Fu man to forget about himself and follow his opponent (strength) instead of himself; that he does not move ahead but responds to the fitting influence. The basic idea is to defeat the opponent by yielding to him and using his own strength. That is why a Gung Fu man never asserts himself against his opponent, and never being in frontal opposition to the direction of his force. When being attacked, he will not resist, but will control the attack by swinging with it. This law illustrates the principles of non-resistance and non-violence which were founded on the idea that

57

the branches of a fir tree snapped under the weight of the snow, while the simple reeds, weaker but more supple, can overcome it. . . . Lao-tzu pointed to us the value of gentleness. Contrary to common belief, the Yin principle, as softness and pliableness, is to be associated with life and survival. Because he can yield, a man can survive. In contrast, the Yang principle which is assumed to be rigorous and hard, makes a man break under pressure.'

To make his point, Bruce then quotes some stanzas from Lao-tzu:

Alive, a man is supple, soft;
In death, unbending, rigorous.
All creatures, grass and trees, alive
Are plastic but are pliant too
And dead, are friable and dry.

Unbending rigor is the mate of death,
And yielding softness, company of life;
Unbending soldiers get no victories;
The stiffest tree is readiest for the axe.
The strong and mighty topple from their place;
The soft and yielding rise above them all

'The way of movement in Gung Fu is closely related to the movement of the mind. In fact, the mind is trained to direct the movement of the *body*. The mind wills and the *body* behaves. As the mind is to direct the bodily movements, the way to control the mind is important; but it is not an easy task . . .

'To perform the right technique in Gung Fu, physical loosening must be continued in a mental and spiritual loosening, so as to make the mind not only agile but free. In order to accomplish this, a Gung Fu man has to remain quiet and calm, and to *master* the principle of 'no-mindedness' . . . *not* a blank mind which excludes all emotions; nor is it simply calmness and quietness of mind. Although quietude and calmness are important, it is the 'non-graspingness' of the mind that mainly constitutes the principle of 'no-mindedness'. A Gung Fu man employs his mind as a mirror —it grasps nothing, and it refuses nothing; it receives, but does not keep . . . Let the mind think what it likes without interference by the separate thinker or ego within oneself. So long as it thinks what it wants, there is absolutely no effort in letting it go; and the disappearance of the effort to let go is precisely the disappearance of the separate thinker. There is nothing to try to do, for whatever comes up moment by moment is accepted, including non-acceptance . . . It is mind immune to emotional influences. . . . No-mindedness is to employ the whole mind as we use the eyes when we rest them upon various objects but make no special effort to take anything in. . . . Therefore, concentration in Gung Fu does not have the usual sense of restricting the attention to a single sense object, but is simply a quiet awareness of whatever happens to be here and now. Such concentration can be illustrated by an audience at a football game; instead of a concentrated attention on the player who has the ball, he has an awareness of the whole football field. In a similar way, a Gung Fu man's mind is concentrated by not dwelling on any particular part of the opponent. This is especially true when dealing with many opponents. For instance, suppose ten men are attacking him, each in succession ready to strike him down. As soon as one is disposed of, he will move on to another without permitting the mind to "stop" with any. However rapidly one blow may follow another he leaves no time to intervene between the two. Every one of the ten will thus be successively and successfully dealt with. . . The flow of thought is like water filling a pond, which is always ready to flow off again. . . .'

'During sparring, a Gung Fu man learns to forget about himself and follows the movement of his opponent, leaving his mind free to make its own countermovement without any interfering deliberation. He frees himself from all mental suggestions of resistance, and adopts a supple attitude. His actions are all performed without self-assertion; he lets his mind remain spontaneous and ungrasped. As soon as he

Bruce Lee's fighting style was all his own.

stops to think, his flow of movement will be disturbed and he is immediately struck by his opponent . . .'

In the following years as fate was to whirl him into unique and demanding environments, Bruce's thinking necessarily became more flexible. He was able to adapt and fit into his changing life-style.

'The world' wrote Bruce, 'is full of people who are determined to be somebody or give trouble. They want to get ahead, to stand out. Such ambition has no use for a Gung Fu man, who rejects all forms of self-assertiveness and competition.

'A Gung Fu man, if he is really good, is not proud at all. Pride emphasises the importance of the superiority of one's status in the eyes of others. There is fear and insecurity in pride because when one aims at being highly esteemed, and having achieved such status, he is automatically involved in the fear of losing his status. Then protection of one's status appears to be his most important need, and this creates anxiety.

'As we know that Gung Fu is aiming at self-cultivation; and, therefore, the inner self is one's true self; so in order to realize his true self, a Gung Fu man lives without being dependent upon the opinion of others. Since he is completely self-sufficient he can have no fear of not being esteemed. A Gung Fu man devotes himself to being self-sufficient, and never depends upon the external rating by others for his happiness. A Gung Fu master, unlike the beginner, holds himself in reserve, is quiet and unassuming, without the least desire to show off. Under the influence of Gung Fu training his proficiency becomes spiritual and he himself, grown ever freer through spiritual struggle, is transformed. To him, fame and status means nothing.'

When he wrote those words, of course, even Bruce had no inkling of what the future held in store for him. He had known fame of a kind since he was a child. But he had little idea of the heights to which he would rise; that he would become a kind of messiah to his own people—an extraordinary combination of Muhammad Ali, Valentino or Clint Eastwood and the Pope; a man worshipped in Hong Kong and in South-East Asia as the embodiment of all the heroic virtues of the Chinese and other Oriental peoples.

He never really consciously set out to achieve the fame and status which, in fact, eventually came his way; which does not mean, however, that he was not conscious of the need to earn a livelihood nor that he did not dream of making the world more conscious of his beloved kung fu. In a letter written to an old friend in Hong Kong in September, 1962, before he had broken into acting in Hollywood, Bruce reveals not only his ~~.~bitions for the future but his determination to make the art of kung fu more widely known.

'This letter is hard to understand. It contains my dreams and my ways of thinking. As a whole, you can call it my way of life. It will be rather confusing as it is difficult to write down exactly how I feel. Yet I want to write and let you know about it. I'll do my best to write it clearly and I hope that you, too, will keep an open mind in this letter, and don't arrive at any conclusions till you are finished.

'There are two ways of making a good living. One is the result of hard working, and the other, the result of the imagination (requires work, too, of course). It is a fact that labor and thrift produce a competence, but fortune, in the sense of wealth, is the reward of the man who can think of something that hasn't been thought of before. In every industry, in every profession, ideas are what America is looking for. Ideas have made America what she is, and one good idea will make a man what he wants to be.

'One part of my life is Gung fu. This art influences greatly in the formation of my character and ideas. I practice gung fu as a physical culture, a form of mental training, a method of self-defense, and a way of life. Gung Fu is the best of all martial art; yet the Chinese derivatives of judo and karate, which are only basics of Gung Fu, are flourishing all over the U.S. This so happens because no one has heard of this supreme art; also there are no competent instructors. . . . I believe my long years of practice back up my title to become the first instructor of this movement. There are yet long years ahead of me to polish my techniques and character. My aim, therefore, is to establish a first Gung Fu Institute that will later spread out all over the U.S. (I have set a time limit of 10 to 15 years to complete the whole project). My reason in doing this is not the sole objective of making money. The motives are many and among them are: I like to let the world know about the greatness of this Chinese art; I enjoy teaching and helping people; I like to have a well-to-do home for my family; I like to originate something; and

62

the last but yet one of the most important is because Gung Fu is part of myself.

'I know my idea is right, and, therefore, the results would be satisfactory. I don't really worry about the reward, but to set in motion the machinery to achieve it. My contribution will be the measure of my reward and success.

'Before he passed away, some asked the late Dr. Charles P. Steinmetz, the electrical genius, in his opinion "What branch of science would make the most progress in the next twenty-five years?" He paused and thought for several minutes then like a flash replied, "spiritual realization". When man comes to a conscious vital realization of those great spiritual forces within himself and begins to use those forces in science, in business, and in life, his progress in the future will be unparalleled.

'I feel I have this great creative and spiritual force within me that is greater than faith, greater than ambition, greater than confidence, greater than determination, greater than vision. It is all these combined. My brain becomes magnetized with this dominating force which I hold in my hand.

'When you drop a pebble into a pool of water, the pebble starts a series of ripples that expand until they encompass the whole pool. This is exactly what will happen when I give my ideas a definite plan of action. Right now I can project my thoughts into the future. I can see ahead of me. I dream (remember that practical dreamers never quit). I may now own nothing but a little place down in a basement, but once my imagination has got up a full head of steam, I can see painted on a canvas of my mind a picture of a fine, big five or six-story Gung Fu Institute with branches all over the States. . . . I am not easily discouraged, readily visualize myself as overcoming obstacles winning out over setbacks, achieving "impossible" objectives.'

Bruce then relates the old Hindu legend where the Supreme Being decided to implant 'the God-head' inside man himself 'because man will never think to look for it within himself'. He then goes on:

'Whether it is the God-head or not, I feel this great force, this untapped power, this dynamic something within me. This feeling defies description, and no experience with which this feeling may be compared. It is something like a strong emotion mixed with faith, but a lot stronger.

'All in all, the goal of my planning and doing is to find the true meaning in life—peace of mind. I know that the sum of all the possessions I mentioned does not necessary add up to peace of mind; however, it can be if I devote to real accomplishment of self rather than neurotic combat. In order to achieve this peace of mind, the teaching of detachment of Taoism and Zen proved to be valuable. . . .

'Probably, people will say I'm too conscious of success. Well, I am not. You see, my will to do spring from the knowledge that I CAN DO. I'm only being natural, for there is no fear or doubt inside my mind. Pearl, success comes to those who become success-conscious. If you don't aim at an object, how the heck on earth do you think you can get it?'

So that by the time he met me, Bruce had a pretty clear idea of the kind of future he wanted, how he was going to achieve it and how to reconcile his ambitions and dreams and whatever success came his way with the underlying principles of kung fu.

By late 1963, Bruce had issued a prospectus for his Institute and was installed in University Way. The regular fee was twenty-two dollars per month and seventeen for juniors. The prospectus, which was printed and illustrated, warned that Gung Fu could *not* be mastered in three easy lessons. Intelligent thinking and hard work were required. Emphasizing the simplicity of the art, Bruce promised that 'techniques are smooth, short, and extremely fast; they are direct, to the point and are stripped down to their essential purpose without any wasted motions'. He promised that Gung Fu would develop confidence, humility, coordination, **adaptability** and *respect* for others.

Under the sub-heading 'Organized despair', he voiced the principal differences between his teaching and that of other martial art instructors. 'Most systems of martial art accumulate "fancy mess" that distort and cramp their pratitioners [sic] and distract them from the actual reality of combat, which is *simple* and *direct*. Instead of going immediately to the heart of things, flowery forms (organized despair) and artificial techniques are ritually presented to simulate actual combat. Thus instead of "being" in combat these pratitioners [sic] are "doing" something "about" combat. Worse still, super mental power and spiritual this and spiritual that are desperately incorparated [sic] until these pratitioners [sic] are drifting further and further into the distance of mystery and abstraction that what they do resembles anything from acrobatics to modern dancing but the actual reality of combat.'

Suddenly Bruce himself found a much more violent form of combat threatening him; induction into the armed services; possible service in Vietnam. Bruce, I believe, would have been a disaster as a soldier or airman and I feel certain he would have ended up being dishonorably discharged or something. He hated routine and had a minimum of patience. While at the university, training in the Armed Services Reserve had been compulsory but he had skipped so many marching exercises that he finally had to get up at four a.m. and march for hours to make up for the time lost. On one occasion, Bruce was chewing gum while marching and the sergeant told him 'Swallow that, soldier!' but instead of obeying, he spat it out and when the sergeant glowered at him, he grinned, 'It's bad for my health!' After the exercise, the sergeant approached Bruce and warned him, 'The next time I say, "Swallow, soldier", you'd better swallow!' Bruce had a few coarse words at his command and he now used them—adding that if the sergeant ever spoke like that to him again, he'd put him on his back! Instead of putting Bruce on a charge, the sergeant walked away, shaking his head as if to say, 'Poor misguided kid.'

The crisis arose when Bruce decided to make a flying trip to see his family in Hong Kong. According to his old English teacher, Mrs. Walters, the draft board were determined that Bruce should not leave the United States. 'They were sure he was going to "skip the ship" and so Bruce had me writing letters and Dean Riley was trying to pull wires to assure them that Bruce Lee was a reputable and honorable gentleman and was not going to skip the country. So finally he got to go to Hong Kong and when he came back, he told us of his visit. He brought me some minor trinket as a present and he showed me a very beautiful gold bracelet he had bought. I see now that he brought this as an eventual present for Linda.'

The draft authorities took away Bruce's student deferment and when he returned to Seattle in September 1963, he was ordered to report for a medical examination. Some ten or twelve University of Washington fellows had to report at the same time. Only two of them could be described as really fit and athletic—Bruce and a football player; and both failed! Bruce, who could toss men weighing two hundred pounds over his shoulder or throw them into the corner of a room with a one-inch punch, was categorized as 4-F! In view of his tragic death, I think it as well to set the record straight here. It has been reported that Bruce was turned down because his arches were too high. In fact, his complaint was an undescended testicle.

Less than a year later, we were married and were on our way to Oakland. Ahead lay an exciting period of struggle, of hard work and frustration, phases of high euphoria and moments of near-despair and despondency. There were times when we were not to have a lot of money; times when it seemed that success was just around the corner. In many ways it was an unsettling life—we moved from house to house no fewer than eleven times in our nine-year marriage. Yet we were never really hard up and just being with Bruce was more than enough for me. We had our years of struggle—but it was a welcome struggle. For Bruce had goals, ambitions and achievements to be realized and knew that for these to become realities he had to put as much into life as he expected to gain from it.

In marriage to Bruce I found all I had ever hoped for. We were entirely different in temperament. Bruce was brilliant, volatile and, in general, the complete extrovert. I think most people regard me as quiet, sensitive—and pay me the compliment of saying I am intelligent. I was certainly not the type of beauty which Bruce had usually dated before our marriage. But I could give him repose, tranquillity, understanding and true love. Whenever we thought about the matter at all, we agreed that together we were the personification of the Double Fish symbol—Yin and Yang.

FIVE

Our first home together was in James Lee's house in Oakland, California. It was a fortunate move in many respects for shortly after we moved in, poor James' wife died, leaving him with two young children on his hands. I was very happy to help out, looking after the children and keeping house. Some show business writers have exaggerated our poverty at this time. In fact, the Jun Fan Institute which Bruce and James established on Broadway initially proved quite successful. Certainly, Bruce never made more than a few hundred dollars a month but our outgo was low.

From the outset of his career, Bruce had to cope with enemies—with men for whom the status quo was sacrosanct. Opposition, in fact, arose from the most unexpected quarters. Until Bruce began to teach it, kung fu was an almost secret art, cherished by the Chinese. The origins of the art, as I have said earlier, are shrouded in mystery and yet certainly the secrets of unarmed combat were known to classical Europe; ancient Greek and Roman boxers, for example, used to break stones with their hands the way modern karate experts break bricks. In China itself, the art is usually traced back to the Shaolin Temple in Honan province, central China, although there is evidence that it was brought to China first by Buddhist monks from India in the third and fourth centuries A.D. and some historians believe it arrived in India with Alexander the Great. Certainly, temple-boxing, as it was called, did not become widely popular in China until the Shaolin Temple of Buddhist monks was destroyed in A.D. 575 by Imperial troops and the monks scattered. As it was a troubled time, the monks, who had developed the basic kung fu movements as a form of exercise, taught their method to the local people so that they could protect themselves against corrupt officials and rampaging bandits. This version of self-defense was probably the 'soft' type. The 'hard' type appears to have been developed in Northern China, possibly Mongolia, and is a much more 'offensive' and aggressive type of fighting. In general the Northern stylists put more emphasis on the leg arts, darting in swiftly to attack and moving out fast, utilizing dramatically high leaps and jumps and high kicks, as well as acrobatic flips and somersaults. In general, the Southern styles favor a deep defensive stance with legs further apart, and with the fighter using short punches and low kicks. Perhaps the most famous of the Northern styles is the Eagle Claw system. This embodies a series of claw-like rakes to the eyes for gouging, or clutching at the throat for choking. The originator of this system was allegedly a general called Yuen Fei, who lived from A.D. 1103–1141. With its striking, clawing and some throwing, this style is not unlike modern ju-jitsu and Aikido. During the Ming Dynasty (A.D. 1368–1644), however, a monk called Lai Cheun combined the Eagle Claw with a style he had developed himself called 'Faan Tzi'. This system is a spectacular one with magnificent high leaps and kicks. Altogether, there are probably five hundred different styles or systems of kung fu—an art which spread to Okinawa about four hundred years ago and thence to Japan, where it became known as karate and ju-jitsu as late as 1917.

Although kicking boxing is also known in Thailand and in Europe, the extraordinary refinements subtleties and range known as the kung fu systems are unquestionably Chinese in their modern forms. For good historical reasons, the Chinese have been always reluctant to divulge these secrets to foreigners. In the last century, Chinese immigrants to California and other Western States were often the subjects of merciless pogroms by Caucasians who saw these gentle, hard-working, pig-tailed people as the advance guard of The Yellow Peril —and, what was more to the point, cheap labor. China itself was subject to increasing foreign exploitation, particularly by the British, from 1870 onwards and secret societies, practicing kung fu and other martial arts, were formed to help eject the 'foreign devils' from the ancient land. Pupils were led to believe that those who had mastered kung fu could overcome anything and a kind of holy frenzy took hold of young men who believed that they could defeat foreign bombs and bullets with only their bare fists and scything legs. Some instructors even fired blanks to 'prove' to their pupils that bullets could not hurt them; it was in this spirit then, that at the beginning of this century, thousands of young Chinese tackled the armies of the advanced industrial powers, including the British and American, in the uprising known as the Boxer Rebellion. And, of course, they were slaughtered by the thousands.

Since then—and the attitude is understandable— Chinese, particularly in America, have been reluctant to disclose these secrets to Caucasians. It became an unwritten law that the art should be taught only to Chinese. Bruce considered such thinking completely outmoded and when it was argued that white men, if taught the secrets, would use the art to injure Chinese, pointed

69

Bruce Lee
ready for action.

out that if a white man really wanted to hurt a Chinese, there were plenty of other ways he could do it. 'After all, he's bigger.'

However, Bruce soon found that at first his views were not shared by members of the Chinese community in San Francisco, particularly those in martial arts' circles. Several months after he and James Lee had begun teaching, a kung fu expert called Wong Jack Man turned up at Bruce's *kwoon* on Broadway. Wong had just recently arrived in San Francisco's Chinatown from Hong Kong and was seeking to establish himself at the time, all his pupils being strictly pure Chinese. Three other Chinese accompanied Wong Jack Man who handed Bruce an ornate scroll announcing a challenge in Chinese. Bruce read the scroll which appears to have been an ultimatum from the San Francisco martial arts

community. Presumably, if Bruce lost the challenge, he was either to close down his Institute or stop teaching Caucasians. Bruce looked at Wong Jack Man:

'Is this what you want?'

Wong Jack Man seemed almost apologetic. 'Well, no, this is not what I want—but I'm representing these people here,' and he indicated his Chinese comrades.

'OK, then,' said Bruce.

This had an extraordinary effect on Wong Jack Man and his supporters—about another half-dozen of their men had now drifted in. Obviously they had imagined that Bruce was a paper tiger—that faced with an actual challenge by a skilled practitioner like Wong Jack Man, he would simply chicken out. They went into what I can only describe as a huddle. When it broke up, Wong Jack Man suggested to Bruce: 'Let's not make this a match—let's just spar together. Let's just try out our techniques.'

Bruce swept this aside impatiently and angrily. Few men had a quicker temper.

'No, you challenged me. So let's fight.'

This flung them all into a tizzy; a real fight was obviously the last thing either they or Wong had reckoned with. So they decided to try and negotiate some rules that would at least save their man a beating.

'No hitting on the face. No kicking in the groin—' began Wong Jack Man.

'I'm not standing for any of that!' declared Bruce. 'You've come here with an ultimatum and a challenge, hoping to scare me off. You've made the challenge—so I'm making the rules. So far as I'm concerned, it's no holds barred. It's all out.'

At that moment, I was over eight months pregnant with Brandon, our son. I suppose I ought to have been nervous. Yet the truth is that I could not have been calmer. I was not in the least concerned for Bruce; I was absolutely certain that he could take care of himself. I may even have smiled a little, realizing that none of these men, apparently, had any real inkling of how dangerous Bruce really could be. The two men came out, bowed formally and then began to fight. Wong adopted a classic stance whereas Bruce, who at the time was still using his Wing Chun style produced a series of straight punches.

Within a minute, Wong's men were trying to stop the fight as Bruce began to warm to his task. James Lee warned them to let the fight continue. A minute later, with Bruce continuing the attack in earnest, Wong began to backpedal as fast as he could. For an instant, indeed, the scrap threatened to degenerate into farce as Wong actually turned and ran! But Bruce pounced on him like a springing leopard and brought him to the floor where he began pounding him into a state of demoralization.

'Is that enough?' shouted Bruce.

'That's enough!' pleaded Wong in desperation.

Still highly incensed, Bruce allowed the man to rise and then threw the whole bunch off the premises. I don't think I've ever seen a more startled or frightened crowd of 'paper tigers'.

The San Francisco martial arts community never again dared to threaten Bruce directly. But a year later, Al Dacascos, who had opened a martial arts school of his own in San Francisco and, like Bruce, had begun teaching Caucasians, was also threatened in a similar way and had to take similar action. The Chinese clans then tried to create bad blood between Bruce and Al, spreading rumors that each was 'calling the other down'; indeed, at one stage, they circulated the story that Al claimed he had taught Bruce everything he knew—all this in the hope, apparently, that the two men would lose their tempers and put each other out of business. Bruce, I may say, was well aware that certain machinations were being directed against him and, when Al approached him at an international tournament in Los Angeles and pointed out that he had never 'called him down' or uttered anything derogatory about him and that he suspected it was merely some of their own people trying to create bad blood between them because they were both instructing Occidentals. Bruce slapped him on the back and told him to forget it. And the two men shook hands.

As Al Dacascos puts it today: 'And that was the last time either of us had any trouble with the Chinese community. In fact, if you go down into San Francisco's Chinatown today—or any other Chinatown—you'll find that Bruce is the great hero. They'll tell you, "Yeah, Bruce is a Chinaman and he's a great kung fu man!"— and they couldn't be more proud of him!'

Bruce, I must emphasize, never deliberately set out to make enemies but it was, perhaps, inevitable that he should rub a large number of people the wrong way. In his sheer enthusiasm for kung fu, he often appeared to people to be far too cocksure and dogmatic. He could not conceal his zeal for a reformation of the traditional attitudes. For example, he came to scoff at the idea of a separation between the 'hard' and 'soft' schools of kung fu. 'It's an illusion,' he declared. 'You see, in reality gentleness—firmness is one inseparable force of one unceasing interplay of movement. . . . We hear a lot of teachers claiming that their styles are the soft and others claiming that theirs are the hard; these people are clinging blindly to one partial view of the totality. I was once asked by a so-called Chinese kung fu "master"— one of those that really looked the part with beard and all—as to what I thought of Yin (soft) and Yang (firm)? I simply answered "baloney!" Of course, he was quite shocked at my answer and still has not come to the realization that "it" is never two.'

Bruce, eventually, came to christen his own teaching Jeet Kun Do—the Way of the Intercepting Fist; yet he resolutely insisted that it ought never to be described as a 'style'. He thought the word inaccurate in relation to what he was trying to do and once explained, 'Fundamentally all styles claim their methods as being able to cope with "all" types of attacks. That means each and every style is complete and total; in other words, their structure covers all possible lines and angles as well as being capable of retaliating from all angles and lines.

Since all possible lines and angles are covered, whence come all these "different" styles?

'I guess he who claims his style is really different must assume his stance on his head and when he strikes, he must turn and spin three times before doing so. After all, how many ways are there to come in on an opponent without deviating from the natural and direct path? By "different", probably, these instructors go only for straight lines, or maybe just round lines, or maybe only kicking, or maybe even just "looking different"; flapping here and flicking there. To me, styles that cling to one partial aspect of combat are actually in bondage. You see, a chosen method, however exacting, fixes its practitioners in an enclosed pattern. I always say that actual combat is never fixed, has no boundaries or limits, and is constantly changing from moment to moment. All of a sudden, the opponent is "alive" and no longer a co-operative robot. In other words, once "conditioned" in a partialized style, its practitioner faces his opponent through a screen of resistance. In reality, he is merely "performing" his stylized blocks and listening to his own screams.'

Bruce's whole life was an evolving process—and this was never seen to greater effect than in his work with the martial arts. The clash with Wong Jack Man metamorphosed his own personal expression of kung fu. Until this battle, he had largely been content to improvise and expand on his original Wing Chun style but then he suddenly realized that although he had won comparatively easily, his performance had been neither crisp nor efficient. The fight, he realized, ought to have ended with a few seconds of him striking the first blows —instead of which, it had dragged on for three minutes. In addition, at the end, Bruce had felt unusually winded which proved to him that he was in a far from perfect condition. So he began to dissect the fight, analyzing where he had gone wrong and seeking to find ways where he could have improved his performance. It did not take him long to realize that the basis of his fighting art, the Wing Chun style, was insufficient. It laid too much stress on hand techniques, had very few kicking techniques and was, essentially, partial. From his own observations he had long ago realized that most forms of kung fu, karate, tae kwon do and other martial arts were based on styles which were basically incomplete. Each had its own forms, movements and so on and each practitioner went into battle believing that he had all the answers and for that reason he refused to call Jeet Kune Do a 'style' which he felt would be to limit it. As it was, therefore, it possessed neither rules, a set number of forms or movements or a set number of techniques with which to oppose other techniques. Its very essence was self-expression—which demanded a great deal of self-knowledge. It was not, therefore, a way of fighting that could be easily taught. It was about this time, in fact, that Bruce began to think about abandoning his plans to open a chain of gung fu schools throughout America. A year or so later, when he had become famous on American TV, efforts were made by important financial interests to persuade him to change his mind and lend his name and prestige to a chain but Bruce resolutely refused to bargain away his integrity repeating that he would run schools only where he could personally supervise the instruction or have it carried on by such assistant instructors as James Lee or Danny Inosanto or Taky Kimura whom he had trained himself—and this, obviously, precluded any possibility of mass instruction for it would take many years to find the right caliber of instructors and to train them.

The Wong Jack Man fight also caused Bruce to intensify his training methods. From that date, he began to seek out more and more sophisticated and exhaustive training methods. I shall try to explain these in greater detail later but in general the new forms of training meant that Bruce was always doing something, always training some part of his body or keeping it in condition. He tended to train each part of his body separately. He did certain exercises to develop his abdominal region and others for his forearms, to put more power into his punches, and leg exercises and kicking. He also did sit-ups and leg raises, but the main benefit derived from the simple act of continually practicing. He was constantly kicking and punching—everything, in fact, depended upon repetition as with a pianist or other musician who spends hours and hours every day practicing the same notes. Gradually, he came to develop several pieces of equipment that he hoped would help him. I often saw him sit down and draw ideas for special equipment on a piece of paper; he would then get somebody to build the apparatus. He constantly sought more *realistic* equipment, for heavy bags and dummies, after all, cannot fight back. So he tried to develop equipment that would increase reaction speed—equipment that would not come back at him in a set pattern but from different angles, forcing him to change, move, be aware, active. But even the best equipment cannot simulate real combat conditions—which is why he did as much unrehearsed sparring as possible.

Bruce was never orthodox—he was always the innovator; the skeptic; the iconoclast. Right from the beginning, for example, he set his face against the kind of rankings that exist in karate. A few years later, when he had become a nationwide celebrity, he was asked by an interviewer if there were any rankings in gung fu. He

Turn book sideways.
Hold the binding in your left hand.
Flip the pages with your right thumb, and watch

BRUCE LEE FIGHT AGAIN!

77

replied, 'Not in traditional gung fu—however, we have a unique ranking system in our particular style. Actually—and here his intense coal-black eyes began to twinkle—'I should say a ranking system of no ranking. The first rank is a blank circle, which signifies original freedom. The second rank is green and white in the form of the Yin Yang symbol with two curved arrows around it. The third is purple and white, the fourth is gray and white, the fifth is red and white, the sixth is gold and white, the seventh is red and gold, which is our school's emblem, and the eighth rank is the highest, which is a blank circle, the return to the beginning stage. In other words, all the previous rank certificates are useful for is for cleaning up messes.'

The great turning point in Bruce's life arrived when he gave an exhibition of kung fu at an international karate tournament at Long Beach, California in 1964. He, James Lee and Taky Kimura had, for some time, been giving exhibitions and demonstrations at various tournaments all over the western United States. At this time, almost nothing was known about the art and Ed Parker, a well-known Los Angeles karate instructor who had taught several police departments and numbered such film people as Warren Beatty and Robert Wagner among his students, issued an invitation to Bruce. Parker, like many people not well acquainted with Bruce, at first thought he was 'cocky' but decided, once he had seen Bruce in action, that he 'had every right to be—he could make the air pop when he hit'.

Bruce's demonstration was watched by a large crowd which included all the leading West Coast karate black belts and instructors. Most people there that night decided that Bruce had not only something different to offer but possessed a unique personality in his own right. He was star material. As one observer commented, 'He had something the others didn't have—you could see it in the way he explained his art, in the way he talked. He was simply dynamic that night and couldn't help drawing people to him. Even those who didn't train in the arts found themselves listening to him intently.' Luckily Ed Parker filmed Bruce's demonstration—this was to prove a fortunate break.

In the audience that evening was a Hollywood hair stylist named Jay Sebring—later among the victims of the Manson gang when they invaded film director Roman Polanski's home and murdered his wife, Sharon Tate, and other guests. Sebring, who later became a good friend of Bruce's and was instrumental in introducing him to Steve McQueen, one of the first of Bruce's 'celebrity' students (Roman Polanski became another) was highly impressed with Bruce's vi-

tality and presence and, when, a few months later, he was cutting the hair of a TV producer called William Dozier, he mentioned Bruce's name. Dozier had said he was looking for someone to play the role of Charlie Chan's number one son in a new TV series he was planning. Jay mentioned that he had seen Bruce in action and believed Dozier should seriously consider him. He thought he had definite charisma, had a great sense of humor and ought to come across to audiences very well. Dozier took Jay's tip and at once got in touch with Ed Parker, who took his film of Bruce's demonstration over to the 20th Century-Fox studios. Dozier liked what he saw and immediately put in a call to our home in Oakland.

79

Bruce was out when the call came through and I spoke to Dozier. Although I had never heard of him and he didn't tell me what he wanted, it sounded very hopeful and when Bruce phoned him back and Dozier explained that he wanted him for a new TV series, we were both very excited. He flew down to Los Angeles for a screen test and as a result, Bruce was signed to an option. Dozier would have put him under contract immediately had it not been that another of his series, a show called *Batman,* had proved such a success with West Coast TV audiences that the network had decided to let it run. In fact, as things turned out, *Batman* ran for another year and *Number One Son* was never made.

Although he had been in the film business all his life, Bruce had never given serious thought to the idea of breaking into American films. He was convinced that the only parts likely to be available to a Chinese were of the 'ah-so!', chop-chop, pigtail-coolie type and he was determined not to lend his talents to that kind of thing. And it is a measure of what he achieved that he managed to destroy that ancient and prejudiced image and, instead, projected an image of a Chinese who, for once, was not only a hero—and one with whom *western* audiences could identify—but a superhuman being; a veritable Chinese James Bond and then some!

The option offer could not have arrived at a more opportune moment so far as we were concerned. Brandon made his appearance in Oakland in February 1965, a week before Bruce's father died in Hong Kong (both Bruce and I felt happy that on his return to Hong Kong in 1963 Bruce had found his father satisfied with his progress in America and that the two men had had an opportunity to move closer together than ever). The Institute in Oakland was not doing quite as well as either Bruce or James Lee had originally hoped. There was only one real reason for this; Bruce was a perfectionist who was determined to admit only serious and talented pupils whom he felt were worth spending his time on.

From the notes he has left, one can easily see with

what thoroughness and business acumen Bruce had set about the job of making his *kwoon* a success. A student of psychology, he had an instinctive awareness of the kind of thing that would attract customers. He made selling points of the exclusivity of his *kwoon*—that it was limited to honored members only; that it was the only one of its kind in the world; that all lessons were personalized and so on. He listed the motives for taking lessons in kung fu—for good health, for securing the admiration of others, for amusement, self-improvement and, above all, peace of mind. He was able to provide prospective customers

with statistics of crimes such as mugging and rape and other assaults and asked, 'What would *you* do if and when you are attacked? What *can* you do when your loved ones are with you during an unprovoked attack?'

There was never any question but that as American violence increased and more and more men and women thought about equipping themselves with some method of self-defense, that Bruce and James could have made a great deal of money. But to Bruce, this would have meant prostituting his art. He was determined to proceed along the lines he had originally envisaged; that is, to teach every class himself, so far as possible, realizing that it was necessary that each pupil understand that the

81

answers lie within himself. With only himself and James Lee available to put over this message—and it was a difficult enough one for some pupils to grasp—it necessarily meant restricting numbers.

With the prospect of a big break in TV ahead of him, Bruce decided that we should move down to Los Angeles immediately. Twentieth Century-Fox arranged that he take a few acting lessons from a coach called Jeff Cory—the only formal training Bruce ever had; basically, he was 'a natural'. The option money amounted to eighteen hundred dollars; a pleasant windfall, if hardly enough to live on for very long. So Bruce opened his third *kwoon* at 628 College Street, Los Angeles. Danny Inosanto, who became his assistant instructor, says: 'Bruce never liked to commercialize his art—so he just painted the windows red. He didn't like signs outside the door and that sort of thing.' What struck Danny most about Bruce as an instructor was how totally relaxed he was, constantly making jokes and keeping everyone in good humor yet at the same time 'keeping good discipline'.

Partly as a joke, but mainly in order to get his message across more graphically, Bruce erected a miniature tombstone near the front door. This was adorned with flowers and inscribed on the tombstone were the words: 'In memory of a once fluid man, crammed and distorted by the classical mess'. Bruce once told *Black Belt* magazine, 'That expresses my feelings perfectly.'

In the notebooks he has left, I have come across the following observations: 'The classical man is just a bundle of routines, ideas and traditions. When he acts he is translating every living moment in terms of the old. To express yourself in freedom, you must die to everything of yesterday. If you follow the classical pattern, you're understanding the routines, the traditions; you are not understanding yourself.'

Again: 'The second-hand artist—in blindly following the *sensei* or *sifu* accepts his pattern and as a result his action and above all his thinking becomes mechanical, his responses automatic according to the pattern—and thereby ceases to expand or to grow. He is a mechanical robot, a product of thousands of years of propaganda and conditioning. One must be uninfluenced and die to one's conditioning in order to be aware of the totally fresh, totally new. Because reality changes every moment, even as I say it.'

Many of these realizations sprang from his reading and subsequent understanding of the forces of nature; others were the product of his own experiences. Once he realized the physical limitations of the Wing Chum style, he rapidly began to branch out, to explore, to test new movements, to re-think the traditional styles. He did not do this by jumping about from style to style or instructor to instructor, but rather by searching inwardly for the best within himself, rejecting the unsuitable and retaining the appropriate. He may have found this easier than most people because he had always felt a personal obligation to himself to be the best at whatever he did—not the biggest or most successful—but rather to express himself to the highest degree of which he was capable. His goal was never to be wealthy or famous but to produce quality work. And, in the end, he managed to arrange his life so that it became like his—Jeet Kune Do—simple, direct, effective. In fighting he achieved this by never being bound by rules or limitations—indeed, he made the slogan of his

Institutes 'Using no way as the way; having no limitation as limitation'. He used to insist when instructing his pupils. 'Efficiency is anything that scores'—and in living, efficiency meant to him to be clear-thinking, always making sure that his thoughts were directed towards purposeful action. For instance, to him it was wrong to wish without moving or to move without having an aim.

Danny Inosanto says, 'The result was that training with Bruce was far more than just learning a way of fighting or of defending yourself. James Lee, for instance, insisted that, after studying with Bruce, he felt morally uplifted, more honest, and that his whole life was changed. Another of Bruce's pupils was, at the start, shy, timid, quiet, and even bashful. Six months later, Bruce had transformed his whole personality. He had learned to fight with all the aggressiveness of a wild animal—and he was able to apply the lessons to ordinary life, coming right out of his shell and blossoming as an individual.'

But how, exactly did Bruce achieve such results?

Danny Inosanto explains, 'Bruce always tailored his instruction to the personality of the person he was talking to. What he would tell one student—or even an assistant instructor—was always different from what he told another. He thus established a very immediate and intimate link with you. He related everything to a personal basis, taking into consideration a person's height, speed, and so on. Some people kicked fast, others slow, some were better with the hand. So he taught each man to find out his own strengths and to use them. He taught everyone to recognize his own weaknesses, too. He explained also that it was no use any of us trying to copy him. None of us possessed his speed, his rhythm, his flexibility, his timing or even his build. He insisted, "Man, because he is a creative individual, is far more important than any style or system." What he set out to do was to liberate people—to liberate them from their own inhibitions. He was both a psychologist and a philosopher—and the students reaped the benefit. I soon

84

realized that I had been preventing myself from achieving my best by being all tensed up and tightened up. The first thing I learned was to free myself from mental tension.'

Many of his students —among them were well-known martial artists and national karate champions in their own right—were convinced that Bruce had a sixth sense. Louis Delgado once described Bruce as 'quite baffling—almost as though he had ESP'. I know that I myself was continually impressed by Bruce's perceptions; I often used to try to catch him off-guard by making a quick movement when he seemed to be im-

mersed in a book or even watching TV, but I always failed. Yet Bruce himself pooh-poohed such nonsense. He told his students, 'Don't disregard your five natural senses in the search for a so-called sixth. Just develop your five natural senses.' He emphasized that all he had done personally was to raise his own senses to their highest pitch.

Danny Inosanto makes the point that Bruce 'really set new standards. He was like a Roger Bannister—like an Einstein, Edison or Leonardo, if you like, so far as the martial arts were concerned.'

Another friend insists, 'Bruce was never pompous, either. Oh, sure, he had human weaknesses—like he wanted admiration and he wanted respect. But he got both from people without any difficulty because he earned them. And although he lived, ate, drank and dreamed martial arts, he wasn't *only* martial arts. Certainly, they dominated his life and overspilled into all his activities—but I can remember whole nights when we all sat around together, listening to Bruce talking and cracking jokes and nobody even mentioned the martial arts. He was never restrictive.'

Our affairs seemed to be going so well, indeed, and our prospects appeared so bright that Bruce decided to spend some of the option money on a trip to Hong Kong. He wanted his mother and family to meet me and Brandon—whom, with a chuckle, he later came to call, 'the only blond, gray-eyed Chinaman in the world'. Everyone made me feel welcome but I found the trip uncomfortable and rather exhausting. There were still so many people living in the Nathan Road flat and the climate seemed impossible—hot and humid and with nowhere to go to get away from it all. Worse, Brandon suffered all the ills usually associated with childhood—everything from colic to a heat rash. I wasn't all that fond of the food either (although now I think there's nothing better) and I found it difficult to make satisfactory contact with some of Bruce's friends and relatives who spoke no English while I understood no Cantonese.

We waited for word from Dozier but all we learned was that everything had been postponed. The only encouraging note was that he did seem definitely to have something in mind for Bruce.

We returned to Seattle in late 1965 and then stayed with James Lee in Oakland until well into the New Year. It was March 1966 before we returned to Los Angeles, where we at once moved into a tiny apartment along Wilshire Boulevard. The *Number One Son* idea had been definitely given the chop by this time, but Dozier was hoping to go into production shortly with a show called *The Green Hornet*. Twentieth Century-Fox wanted to let *Batman* run for one season to test the audience reaction before beginning *The Green Hornet*.

Based on one of the most successful American radio serials of the 1930s, *The Green Hornet* was intended to show the exploits of Britt Reid, a crusading newspaper editor-publisher who donned green clothes at night and turned crime-fighter. As Kato, his manservant and assistant, Bruce was to catapult to stardom overnight in America. Later Bruce cracked to a newspaper interviewer: 'The only reason I ever got that job was because I was the only Chinaman in all California who could pronounce Britt Reid.'

SIX

The Green Hornet was destined to become one of the more forgettable shows on American TV—which may be saying a lot. Yet even before the show premiered, it became clear that if any person or anything about it had a chance of capturing the public imagination, it was Bruce and the art of gung fu.

Bruce made several personal appearances around the

country in preparation for the first screening of the series. He made a stunning impression, a Minneapolis critic going so far as to write: 'I can tell the producers of *The Green Hornet* how to improve their show—even before it's on the air. What they should do is let the Hornet's sidekick, Kato, write his own dialogue. He's bright and he's funny.'

In fact, the show lasted for about thirty episodes only during the 1966–67 season (there were numerous reruns, however). Bruce later explained that he thought the series had been played too 'straight' to capture a big adult audience and that 'a lighter James Bond touch with more time and fewer characters would have helped' —Britt Reid and Kato never had more than a half hour to run their villains to earth and for a considerable part of that time, the screen was simply cluttered with people. But although adults found the stories corny and farfetched, children everywhere loved Bruce. Even the most scathing critics admitted that Bruce's gung fu was sensational. One critic wrote: 'Those who watched him would bet on Lee to render Cassius Clay senseless if they were put in a room and told that anything goes.'

Everyone was impressed by the sheer speed of Bruce's movements—'He strikes with such speed that he makes a rattler look like a study in slow motion', wrote one reviewer. In fact, Bruce had to explain to interviewers that he was forced to pull his punches and slow down his movements, so that the camera could catch his actions. 'At first, it was ridiculous,' he explained. 'All you could see were people falling down in front of me. Even when I slowed down, all the camera showed was a blur.'

He told one interviewer, 'One of the main characteristics will be the speed of the fights and the simplicity in finishing off the Hornet's enemies.' Bruce, I must emphasize again, was a showman; he knew as much about showmanship—as his careful notes on 'selling' his lessons show—as Barnum and Bailey. But there was a limit to how far he would exploit his art. Chinese films —made at Run Run Shaw's Hong Kong factory—

tended to stage long drawn-out battles to achieve the maximum effect of gore and violence. Bruce, instead, insisted that on any level—not only on the effective but artistic — a u d i e n c e s would be far more impressed with the sudden, deadly strike, the overwhelming, annihilating effect of gung fu. Provided the essence of his own expression was retained, he was prepared to allow a certain poetic or theatrical license—which was why viewers saw him perform flying jumps he would never indulge in in real life.

As another interviewer wrote: 'The object of gung fu is to send a foe to the nearest hospital in the shortest possible time, what Lee calls "a maximum of anguish with a minimum of movement". This is accomplished with knees, elbows, fingers in the eyes, feet in the teeth.' The same interviewer managed, I think, to catch part of the essence of Bruce's multi-sided character and personality when he added: 'When he isn't playing the cold-eyed Kato, Lee is the complete ham, alternately the pixie and the tough kid down the block. He puns unmercifully, performs dazzling feats of speed and coordination, wades bravely into the riptides of a language he is trying to master. Sample Lee wit: "Seven hundred million Chinese cannot be Wong", "I don't drink or smoke. But I do chew gum, because Fu Man Chu." '

When anybody is as outspoken as Bruce, of course, controversy is bound to follow in his wake. 'Ninety-nine per cent of the whole business of Oriental self-defense is baloney,' he declared to reporters. 'It's fancy jazz. It looks good, but it doesn't work. If a ninety-pound woman is attacked by a two-hundred-and-fifty-pound man, the only thing she can do is strike hard at one of three places—the eyeballs, the groin or the shins. This should be sufficient to put the man off-balance for just a moment and then she'd better run like hell.

'Or this matter of breaking bricks and boards with the edge of your hand. How often, I ask you, did you ever see a brick or a board pick a fight with anybody? This is gimmick stuff. A human being doesn't just stand there and wait to be hit.' So many karate students were wrapped up in the snorting sounds and the counter moves he insisted that they lost sight of what they should be doing to an opponent—'getting him out of there, quick. The karate teacher says "if your opponent does this, then you do this, and then you do this and then you do this." And while you are remembering the "and thens", the other guy is killing you. Faced with the choice of socking your opponent in the head or poking him in the eyes, you go for the eyes every time.'

Asked what kind of people became students at his *kwoons,* he explained, 'People from every walk of life. Some want to lose weight. Some say they want to be able to defend themselves. But I would say that the majority are there for one reason—vanity. It is exotic. They figure they'll learn Zen and meditation. I say that if you want something beautiful, you should take up modern dancing. What good would it do a boxer to learn to meditate? He's a fighter, not a monk. It's all too ritualistic, what with bowing and posturing. That sort of Oriental self-defense is like swimming on land. You can learn all the swimming strokes, but if you're never in the water, it's nonsense. These guys never *fight.* They all want to break three-inch boards or two bricks or something. Why? That doesn't make them fighters.'

Such statements were controversial enough—and it's

perhaps useless to deny that many other martial arts instructors must have felt highly annoyed with Bruce, although the very best of them, such as Jhoon Rhee, however much they disagreed with Bruce, respected him for his honest views and integrity and became his life-long friends. His use of nunchakus, however, led to other kinds of criticism. These are two rods, connected by a piece of leather or chain and are generally used to flair at an opponent in extreme cases one could even strangle an opponent with them). Their use, of course, is banned in many parts of the world and in some states of the U.S. even their  possession is a felony. Bruce, however, was solely concerned with their dramatic and theatrical appeal. His library contained many books about weapons, both ancient and modern, Oriental and Western, and he saw the nunchakus as nothing more than a diverting prop—and no more likely to encourage youngsters to violence than the use of a rifle by John Wayne in a western.

Bruce, like other colorful, larger-than-life personalities, full of zest and almost demonic energy, unquestionably enjoyed the fame and adulation that came from his appearance in *The Green Hornet*. He basked in the sunshine of personal appearances, various openings and he even rode on processional floats dressed in the black suit, chauffeur's cap and black mask of his Kato role. He enjoyed it all and yet was aware that this type of publicity was only superficially rewarding. His real reward was in providing quality performances—all other benefits, even financial gain, were only icing on the cake. Bruce was no plaster saint. He was an extrovert. He was uninhibited. He lived life as though it were always going to end tomorrow. Margaret Walters has made the interesting point that Bruce's intensity, his drive for perfection, the excitement and activity with which he surrounded so much of what he did reminded her of something written by the great German writer, Thomas Mann. This was to the effect that people who were not going to live long apparently had a clock inside them that warned them that they did not have too many years and so they worked hard and tried to do too much in a short time, whereas people who were going to live for a long time had a clock which told them there was no particular hurry.

Bruce could not help being jaunty and excited by life —and excited by his own strength and dynamic power. And he wanted people to share in this excitement. Peter Chin, who was an extra on *The Green Hornet,* recalls that some of the people on the set 'were put off' by Bruce's behavior off-screen. 'He was always showing people his muscles—showing them how strong he was. I couldn't understand why they got so up-tight just because he was strong; just because he wanted to show them what he had been able to do to his body. Not that they ever said anything straight out to him—but when he had walked away, you'd hear someone say, "Oh, he's bullshitting—he's a big loudmouth". But he wasn't—and that's where they missed the point. He *was* strong. He *was* exceptional.'

In my judgment, Bruce was able to keep a pretty detached view of himself. He knew how good he was; he realized how much he was capable of accomplishing— yet he tried to exclude bombast. 'I'll never say I'm number one,' he used to tell me, 'but I'll never admit to being number two.' And he had the saving grace of always being able to laugh at himself. When he was going through a particularly bad period and for once in his life feeling low, he put up a little sign on his desk which simply said, 'Walk on'. For a time he hung a lugubrious poster on the wall showing two vultures in the middle of an otherwise blank desert—blank, that is, save for the skeleton of an old cow and one vulture is saying to the other, 'Patience, my ass! I'm going to *kill something*!'

Yet for all the success and excitement, the adulation and the autograph signing, he continued to nurture the more studious, more scholarly side of his character. He lived by the Yin-Yang principle. He and Danny Inosanto often spent hours together, just rambling around Los Angeles with Bruce driving in and out of bookstores, particularly old bookstores. Very quickly, he built up a colossal library, impelled by a seemingly insatiable desire to learn everything he could about the martial arts in their widest and most far-reaching form. He bought books on swords and other weapons and on combat tactics of every kind; on boxing and wrestling; he wanted a distillation of all that was best and to adapt it to the practice of kung fu or for spectacular action on the screen. He carried a book with him wherever he went—even when he knew he would get little chance to

93

read it. He had, fortunately, developed the ability to shut out distractions. I've seen Bruce sitting quietly reading while there was household uproar all around him—children crying, doors slamming and banging, people coming in to chat or gossip. He could insulate himself against it all, remaining, seemingly, totally oblivious to anything short of an earthquake—his mind concentrated on ideas and actions possibly from some remote period in Chinese history. Bruce was even able to read a book while performing a series of quite strenuous exercises.

Before and after *The Green Hornet,* he spent much of his time giving demonstrations of kung fu. These were at fairs, public parks and club meetings, often for charity, sometimes for money. He showed how to jab with the fingers, how to punch—although he never actually struck anybody—and delivered kicks so fast that anybody in the audience who even blinked probably missed the action. Sometimes he would place his wrists against an opponent's and dare the man to try to prevent him from hitting him on the chest—yet nobody was ever fast enough (he called this 'sticky hands' which is part of Wing Chun training). He sometimes did his one-finger push-ups; kicked and broke *eight* two-inch boards bound together with tape—and even attempted (and succeeded, of course) in public in performing one of the most difficult feats in all martial arts; snapping five one-inch boards dangled in front of him. On the whole he hated this kind of stunt—he considered it 'phony' and having nothing to do with learning how to defend yourself. In fact, although there are genuine exponents of the board or brick breaking techniques—James Lee could smash a brick with the *back* of his hand, a truly extraordinary feat—most expositions are sheer fakes. It is very easy to bake bricks or dry out boards so that they become so brittle that almost anybody could break them (I can do it myself). Bruce rarely indulged in this kind of stunt because of this—but did do it once or twice to *prove* he could do it if he wanted to. But it used to annoy him when he watched other martial artists do it on TV, dismissing the act impatiently, 'What's *that* got to do with fighting?'

Through *The Green Hornet* he first learned what it was to become a public idol—and how frightening that can be sometimes. People fought to get his autograph or even just to touch him. 'It can be a terrifying experience sometimes,' he told *Black Belt* magazine. 'After a personal experience at Madison Square Garden at a karate tournament, I started to make an exit through a side door, escorted by three karate men. I was practically mobbed outside and I had to leave through another side door.' In Fresno, California, he was scratched, kicked and gouged by riotous fans. He admitted himself, 'I just couldn't protect myself. Sixty percent of the fans were young boys but a surprising proportion were young girls. His piercing dark eyes and handsome features, totally lacking that impassivity or inscrutability popularly associated with Chinese by some Americans, was something as fresh and novel in their young lives as kung fu itself, I feel.

All this created a welcome change in our financial affairs, at least. Within a few months of Bruce's dazzling success, I found it almost impossible to remember how low we had been in June 1966 when *The Green Hornet* first went into production. He was paid four hundred dollars a week—and the first check arrived at just the right moment; we hadn't enough to pay the rent and other outstanding bills. Not that Bruce ever showed anything but a sunny and optimistic face to the world. His friend Jhoon Rhee recalls, 'He was a supremely confident person—and if he had worries, he never showed them. I remember once asking him, "Gee, don't you ever get discouraged, Bruce?" He replied, "Of course, I get discouraged—but there's no sense in worrying about things." He definitely thought positive. For instance, when *The Green Hornet* ended and he didn't have a job —at least, wasn't making enough to support his family in the style he wanted them to have—he would become annoyed if someone suggested that "circumstances" were holding him back. "To hell with circumstances." Bruce almost yelled, "I will *make* the circumstances." '

In fact, although we didn't know it then, *The Green Hornet* was to make Bruce quite a bit of money in residuals—domestic re-runs and sales of the series overseas. Eventually we were able to buy a nice house in Upper Bel Air—which was very exciting, for although it was far from being a mansion, indeed, it was a very ordinary house, it was our first real home and that made it rather special. But there was never any question of Bruce suddenly deciding to live it up. Bruce, I should explain, never placed that much importance on possessions. Possessions were not what he wanted from life. Certainly, he wanted *security*—for that spelled independence; and it meant, too, that he could pursue excellence. And it was excellence, quality, achievement, call it what you will, that he really wanted. In a way, of course, he thought of money as something that would accrue to him as a matter of course if he achieved quality. He never felt he could ignore it—but making money wasn't his primary aim. He could see money, possessions and all the rest of the apparatus of success in their true perspectives. For instance, he was never a name dropper—and having lots of famous friends meant absolutely nothing to him. He used to say, 'the

96

best carpenter is just as important as the man who's made an important film'. Even before he became famous, he felt himself the equal of anyone else around him and he never felt any sense of inferiority because he was Chinese or because he wasn't a millionaire. He never looked at life in quite that way. Much of this may have had something to do with the fact that he *knew* he was going to be a great success one day. When we were still relatively poor, he did notice the rich and their life-styles, but he never felt envious of them—one, because I don't think he ever cared whether he could afford nice things or not; two,

because he took it for granted that he would eventually be successful. Certainly, I always had the most tremendous confidence in him. You could almost see the electricity flaring around him. With such drive and ability, I knew that success was inevitable.

Nonetheless, even in the most successful lives and careers, troughs are fairly frequent—and Bruce experienced one after *The Green Hornet*. I suppose, in a sense, going back to teaching at the kwoon, which Danny Inosanto had meantime kept going, must have seemed an anti-climax. And teaching demanded his full-time energies. Bruce, I think, realized that it was time for decisions. There was no way he could run the kwoon full-time and still become a success in show business.

One of the men who came to his assistance with good advice at this juncture was the assistant producer of *The Green Hornet,* Charles Fitzsimon, who became one of his best friends. Bruce used to go and lunch with him at 20th Century-Fox studios and it was from Charles that Bruce got ideas about his film career and about how to make kung fu pay him a satisfactory living wage. Charles suggested that instead of relying on the twenty-two dollars a month Bruce charged for lessons at the kwoon, he should teach students privately—at fifty dollars an hour! Even Bruce was a bit taken back—but Fitzsimon pointed out that Hollywood was full of rich people who would be delighted to pay that sort of money (in fact, Bruce's rates rose to a regular two hundred and fifty dollars an hour—and people like Roman Polanski even flew him to Switzerland for special lessons). Jay Sebring at once put Bruce in touch with Steve McQueen who became his first 'celebrity' pupil. Bruce and Steve hit it off very well together—and Steve loved driving fast—and, as soon as he was able, bought a Porsche himself). Bruce found Steve a very apt pupil—Steve had had a rough childhood himself and was used to juvenile gang fights as a kid—and he quickly picked up the fighting elements of gung fu. Bruce used to say that Steve 'was a fighter' while Jim Coburn 'was a philosopher'. The difference between the two stars was that one was an intensely *physical* man, while the other was far more interested in the philosophy underlying the martial arts. Private instruction eventually became one of Bruce's most lucrative activities. It was during this period that some of the greatest karate men came to him for special instruction. Later, the Washington *Star* was to write, 'Three of Bruce Lee's pupils, Joe Lewis, Chuck Norris and Mike Stone have between them won every major karate championship in the United States. Joe Lewis was grand national champion in three successive years. Bruce Lee handles and instructs these guys almost as a parent would a young child which can be somewhat disconcerting to watch. It's like walking into a saloon in the Old West and seeing the fastest draw in the territory standing there with notches all over his gun. Then in walks a pleasant little fellow who says "How many times do I have to tell you that you're doing it all wrong," and the other guy listens intently.' Louis Delgado told *Black Belt*, 'I have never seen anyone who has baffled me so completely. I am completely in awe when I fight [spar with] him.' Perhaps the greatest t r i b u t e s to Bruce's tuition and mastery came from Chuck Norris and Joe Lewis. Chuck went on TV and stated to millions that Bruce was his teacher and that he considered him 'fantastic' while Joe

Lewis, on being awarded the heavyweight crown, publicly thanked Bruce for the improvement he had made to his fighting. Coming from Joe Lewis, considered a sort of rebel in karate, this was something; but Bruce in fact, showed Joe how to improve his tools to such effect that in a sparring session Joe actually broke three of Bob Wall's (another champion) ribs. Danny Inosanto explains, 'The secret of kicking, as Bruce taught it, was controlled anger. I remember once he asked me to try kicking. He held this shield and for five minutes, I kicked at that shield, desperately trying to improve my kick. I really thought I was giving it my all—but Bruce still wasn't satisfied. Finally, he came over and slapped me on the face—at the same time calling out, "Now kick!" He held up the shield—I was simply blazing with anger and went pow! It was fantastic.' Bruce rarely used this type of incentive in teaching, but he knew Dan's temperament well enough to know it was necessary.

Black Belt carried a long two-part series on Bruce around this time. The interviewer, Maxwell Pollard, noted that Bruce neither smoke nor drank and strove to keep physically fit at all times—starting the day with a mile and a half run with his Great Dane, Bobo, followed by various calisthenics and technique-sharpening exercises and additional workouts in the afternoons. What really impressed Mr. Pollard was that twice during the four hours he spent with Bruce, the latter refused to drink even a cup of coffee. The first time he chose milk, the second a soft drink.

At the *kwoon* in Chinatown, Maxwell had a long talk with Bruce and also watched him work out with Dan Lee, one of Bruce's best friends and a brilliant kung fu man. 'Private lessons are usually not interesting,' Bruce explained. 'It's more enjoyable to teach those who have gone through conventional training. They understand and appreciate what I have to offer. When I find an interesting and potential prospect, I don't charge him a cent (this was true).

The reporter found Bruce moving about the *kwoon* 'like a panther, counterattacking, moving in, punching with great power—occasionally, shin kicks, finger-jabs, powerful body-punches to the solar plexus, use of elbows and knees.' What particularly impressed him was that Bruce's body was constantly relaxed. He thought Bruce's movements those 'of a polished, highly-refined prize-fighter, delivering his blows with subtle economy'. His movements seemed to be a 'mixture of the Wing Chun style and Western fencing'.

By this time, Bruce's expression had so evolved that he had to give it a name of its own—Jeet Kune Do. He explained that *Jeet* meant 'to stop, to stalk, to intercept', *Kune* meant 'fist or style' and *Do* meant 'the way or the ultimate reality'. It was, Bruce explained, 'the direct expression of one's feelings with the minimum of movements and energy. There is no mystery. My movements are *simple, direct* and *non-classical*.' There were no sets or classical forms in the method because *they* tended to be rhythmic—and so when he sparred, he used 'b r o k e n rhythm'. He added, 'classical forms are futile attempts to "arrest" and "fix" the ever-changing m o v e-ments in combat and to dissect and analyze them like a corpse. But when you're in actual combat, you're not fighting a corpse. Your opponent is a living, moving object who is not in a fixed position, but fluid and alive. Deal with him realistically, not as though you're fighting a robot.'

Pollard pressed him to explain what he meant by 'directness'. Almost before the words were out of his mouth, Bruce's wallet had gone flying through the air. Instinctively, Pollard reached up and caught it. Bruce said, 'That's *directness*. You did what comes naturally. You didn't waste time. You just reached up and caught the wallet—and you didn't squat, grunt or go into a horse stance or embark on some such classical move before reaching out for the wallet. You wouldn't have caught it if you had. In other words, if somebody grabs you, punch him! Don't indulge in any unnecessary, sophisticated moves! You'll get clobbered if you do and in a street fight, you'll have your shirt ripped off you.' Bruce then gave what he and I always thought of as a classic definition of Jeet Kune Do: 'In building a statue, a sculptor doesn't keep adding clay to his subject. Actually, he keeps chiseling away at the unessentials until the truth is revealed without obstructions. Jeet Kune Do doesn't mean adding more. It means to minimize. In other words to back away the unessentials. It is not a "daily increase" but a "daily decrease". Art is really the expression of the self. The more complicated and restricted the method, the less the opportunity for the expression of one's original sense of freedom. Though they play an important role in the early stage, the techniques should not be too mechanical, complex or restrictive. If we blindly cling to them, we will eventually become bound by their limitations. Remember, you are *expressing* the techniques and not *doing* the techniques. If somebody attacks you, your response is not Technique No. 1, Stance No. 2, Section 4, Paragraph 5. Instead, you simply move in like sound and echo, without any deliberation.'

James Coburn, who was Bruce's second 'celebrity' pupil, vividly describes what it was like to be a student of Bruce's. He had already been taught karate by an experienced coach for his role in *Our Man Flint*. 'That first day we went out back and we started going through a few punches and things, hits and sidekicks and so on, so that he could find out where I was. We started working in earnest the following week and worked solid three days a week for the next four or five months. Working on two levels at the same time—so that in that time we became very good friends. I was interested more in the esoteric vent while he was immersed in the total—the esoteric and physical. His method of teaching was not teaching at all in the accepted sense—it was evolving through certain ideas; teaching you tools; finding out your strong points, your weak points. Our getting together lasted over four years—I'd have to go away on location at times—but each time I came back, I was astonished to observe how Bruce had evolved even further in the meantime. The steps he had taken in between times were really giant steps.

102

'He always had this energy. It was always exploding on him—though he channeled it whenever possible, which was most of the time. I mean he actually created this energy within himself. He always got more force from doing something, for instance. We'd work out together for an hour and a half and at the end of that time, he'd be filled with force. You really felt high when you finished working out with Bruce. He was always trying to bring everything down to one thing —one easy, simple thing. There are, in fact, no complicated methods in Jeet Kune Do—anyone, really, can do them. But it was the perfection.

We'd do a thing—a thing Bruce called "bridging the gap". It's the distance from your opponent you have to stand in order to score—it's how close you can get in, in other words, and move away fast enough not to get hit in turn. It amounts to constant observation of your opponent and constant observation of yourself, so that you and your opponent are one—not divided. You know, nobody could touch Bruce if he didn't want them to—he was that damn good! He'd let me touch him a couple of times, just so that I could get the feel of it. And while you were picking up this physical "bridging of the gap", you were learning to overcome certain psychological barriers at the same time.

'And the one important point about Bruce—the thing

that needs to be emphasized as much as anything else was that he himself was constantly learning. I don't think a day went by when he wasn't gathering in some new thing. He'd be bursting with enthusiasm about some new kick he'd just invented—"Bang! Bang!—look at that, man! Try it, man!", he'd shout—and I'd try it and it was, well, the flow of energy was always, well, like a whip—always relaxed until right at the end, all the force came out—*tung*!

'So far as kicks were concerned, we did a lot of work with big bags. I remember once I got a brand-new bag—about a hundred pound thing hung up with a big L iron. Bruce thought it was a little too hard—"that's not really the right kind for you," he said, "but we'll work with it today anyway—maybe I can soften it up a bit for you". So he took a running side kick at it and broke the chain! I mean that thing hung on a seventy-five pound chain—and he broke that chain and broke a hole in the canvas —it flew up in the air and fell out in the middle of the lawn out there—busted, dilapidated—a brand-new bag. Wow! And the things he could make you do! I mean he told me there was no trick to breaking boards—that I could easily do it. So he told me "Take off your shoe" and I did so—and then he showed me how to use my heel—and bang! sure enough, it would feel sensational; the board went. Then Bruce would say, "Right, man, now let's get down to some real work, eh?" '

SEVEN

'Some of the struggles Bruce had getting really heavily involved in films read like a scene out of any really grim fight against prejudice. Bruce would never play the chop-chop pigtail coolie. Everyone admired him for that. He insisted on being human.' So said Academy Award winning screenwriter Stirling Silliphant, one of Bruce's best friends and one of the many well-known Hollywood personalities who became his student; a list which also includes James Garner, Elke Sommer, Sy (Tarzan) Weintraub, the producer and Kareem Abdul Jabbar, the basketball hero.

Stirling wrote *Marlowe*, starring James Garner, which was Bruce's first appearance in a Hollywood full-length motion picture. 'Two of the best sequences had Bruce in them,' says Stirling. 'I wrote him into it. In one, he came in and tore up Garner's office. In the other, he met Garner on the roof of the Occidental building and took a header, kicking and screaming off into space.'

Stirling Silliphant never had any doubt that Bruce was star material. But it was one thing spotting star material; another finding the right plots and stories—and the right people to back him with hard finance. In the ordinary Hollywood movie, there are not all that many parts for a Chinese—so something special had to be created for him, but at this stage he still wasn't what the movie people call 'a bankable' property. When Stirling wrote a love story for Columbia called *A Walk in the Spring Rain*, he actually wrote in a fight sequence. But as he explains, 'The problem was that the scene was set in the Tennessee Mountains. Well, there weren't any Orientals in the story, because they just didn't have any Asians down there. But I brought Bruce down to Tennessee to choreograph and stage the fight. There were two stuntmen on the picture. They were very skeptical of Bruce. Here they were, big, tough Caucasian cats, and Bruce weighed in at 135 pounds, a rather gentle and smooth-looking Chinese who wasn't tough. In fact, he always maintained a very cool and low profile. The fellows resented my bringing in an outsider to stage the fight. I made it clear to them that since I was producer and writer of the picture, Bruce was the boss on their fight.

'The guys kept putting Bruce on, so I said, "Why don't you just give them a little sample of what a sidekick can do?" Bruce had the air shield with him because we worked out all the time. So he said, "One of you guys hold this shield. I'm going to give it a little kick. But I suggest you brace yourself first, you know, I kick pretty hard." They went through their "sure, sure" routine. So I told Bruce to make it really interesting and do it by the swimming pool. If those guys are so tough and can take it with their backs to the pool, why okay. But if he kicks as hard as I think he can, and they aren't really braced, well, it'll knock 'em right into the water. Everybody said, "Cool, man". So with no movement, no run, nothing, just standing there in front of the guy, he went, *sshhp!* like that. He kicked this guy right through the air and out into the middle of the pool. Then the other guy had to prove himself, too. So he braced real low. And *sshhp!* again. He kicked this guy, lifted him off his feet, up into the air and out into the pool! Well, that guy came up a Christian! So, from that moment on, those guys loved Bruce.'

All this delightful stuff still lay ahead when *The Green Hornet* folded. With its ending, Bruce had to face a really frustrating and dispiriting time. He knew he was good; knew he must some day make it, yet the days passed and the big breaks still seemed as far away as ever. He spent time with Steve McQueen, getting to know and like him as well as teaching him. They were both a little mad about cars; when Bruce finally got his Porsche, one of the first things Bruce did was to bring it over to Steve's house and give it a thorough check. We even got Riff, our Schnauzer, from the McQueen house. When we first decided to buy our place in Bel Air. Steve came across to look the place over first and even had his business manager check it to make sure that it would be a good investment. Bruce and he saw a fair amount of each other and had a lot of good talks together; at one time they even discussed doing a project

together. They would have made a great combination!

Bruce was never a great socializer; like Steve McQueen, he didn't like parties all that much. Even when he had become one of the greatest box office successes in the world and his photograph was on the front cover of every magazine in the world—or so it sometimes seemed—he didn't spend much of his time at parties. He never drank alcohol and he hated nightclubs. But he and I went along to one or two during his lean period, partly because one never knew what opportunities might suddenly present themselves, partly because the invitations simply came from one of his students, such as Sy Weintraub or Elke Sommer. The trouble with film parties is that the stars want to be at the center of things and Bruce was too much his own man, too conscious of his own worth, to join in the fawning, adulatory chorus that tends to surround the Big Name. Yet, inevitably, at some time during the evening, when I turned round and looked for Bruce, he would be in the center of a group, doing push-ups or performing his coin trick or holding the floor on philosophy or the martial arts. I used to marvel at the look of amazement on everyone's face; particularly when he performed some feat of strength. Americans, after all, expect a Hercules to be a giant of a man; they simply weren't ready for Bruce. And Bruce, on first meeting, was always so polite and courteous— although never self-effacing—that I think most of them got the impression that he was simply there to take away the dishes. The impact he made on the Western mind, therefore—at least in so far as Hollywood represents the Western mind—was startling, almost revolutionary. Amusing, enlightened, novel. Bruce found the doors of hospitality thrown open to him all over Hollywood.

He could easily have picked up large sums of money at this time, following his success as Kato. Very considerable pressure was brought to bear on him to exploit the role with a series of schools directed primarily at the youngsters who had become his greatest fans. Bruce wouldn't listen. Success was one thing—but the integrity of his martial arts was another. He even remained quite firm about the kind of pupils he would accept. Stirling Silliphant still tells how amazed he was at Bruce's reaction when he first approached him about private lessons. Stirling says that it took him months even to get to Bruce, which he found remarkable when he considered that as a writer-producer he often hired actors and Bruce was looking for work as an actor. And —what was even more remarkable—was how, even when they finally managed to meet, Bruce still refused to play the sycophant. Instead of welcoming Stirling with open arms and playing up to him in the hope of favors to come, Bruce told him, 'I think you're too old [Silliphant was forty-nine]. I don't believe there's a chance your reflexes are good enough to do what I want you to do.'

'Well, I did a few things a n d he seemed pleased and rather surprised,' says Stirling, who had been a fencing champion at the University of Southern California and still had incredible eyesight and reflexes. He worked for two years as a student with Bruce and earned two certificates of accomplishment. Stirling says that studying with Bruce changed his whole life; his habits of living and working underwent an utter change. In his writing, his material expanded, his point of view on the human condition became more profound

and he discovered it much easier to touch an audience's emotions. 'What Bruce taught me is still so much with me, almost a kind of growing thing. He was not a teacher—and yet he was the greatest teacher I have ever known.'

With the help of such good friends as Stirling Silliphant, Jim Coburn, Steve McQueen, Sy Weintraub and others—plus, of course, his own natural drive and determination, Bruce kept in the public eye with guest appearances on TV shows such as 'Ironside', 'Blondie' and 'Here Come the Brides'. They all helped, as they say, to pay the rent. Then Stirling and Bruce got together to work on a TV series called *Longstreet*. 'We worked out the opening story together,' says Stirling. 'It was called The Way of the Intercepting Fist; that's a literal translation of the martial art form Bruce originated. James Franciscus starred as the blind detective. Bruce played an antique dealer who saves Jim from being clobbered by some toughs trying to force him off the dock. Of course, the blind man wanted to know how he did what he did. Bruce's character refuses because the motivations of revenge are wrong. So the story dealt with getting the blind detective's head together and learning the way of the intercepting fist. We had more fan mail on that episode than any other in the series. I like to think that that episode was his first good film— the first to show him off to the world as an Oriental martial artist with pride and dignity. We used him three more times, and from there he began to get offers. On that first *Longstreet*, Bruce was shown as a perfect teacher; the mystic simplicity of his lessons really came through. It is still one of the best martial arts shows I've ever seen on the air. I say that even though I wrote the final script. Ted Ashley over at Warner Brothers approached him to do a series, and some films. But first, Bruce went to Hong Kong. There, he translated his magnetism into incredible screen portrayals and came back a superstar.'

Perhaps this show, more than any other, convinced Bruce that his dreams had real validity; that he was not simply deluding himself. He spilled out his fierce conviction in his own ultimate success to anybody who would listen. He had an endearing habit of making prophecies—and so that nobody could ever accuse him of being wise after the event, always committed them to paper. I still have one written about this time (early 1969) which is really quite remarkable. Headed 'My Definite Chief Aim', it says:

'I Bruce Lee, will be the first highest paid Oriental superstar in the United States. In return I will give the most exciting performances and render the best of quality in the capacity of an actor. Starting 1970, I will achieve world fame and from then onward till the end of 1980 I will have in my possession $10,000,000. I will live the way I please and achieve inner harmony and happiness.'

Even Bruce never guessed at the colossal success that awaited him. Had he lived he certainly would have fulfilled his prophecies and more.

In the meantime, while he was waiting for the Hollywood moguls to wake up to his potential, he worked at his martial arts, constantly seeking higher and higher planes of achievement for himself; constantly seeking better ways of inculcating the right attitudes in his students. Ed Parker has expressed a fairly firm

view about Bruce's success as a teacher. He insists that Bruce himself was 'one in two billion' and that God had given him 'all the natural talents.' But, says Parker, his problem as a teacher was that he could pass on his ideas, but not his talent, so that his philosophy failed to work for some of his students. Referring to Bruce's analogy about the sculptor chipping away at the stone. Ed commented, 'But if a guy doesn't have the natural talent Bruce had, he can chip all day and he isn't going to find what *he* had.' The problem of being a successful teacher is hardly one that Bruce alone found difficult; any teacher of *any* subject finds this true. The very essence of Bruce's teaching, in fact, was that what might work

111

for him would not necessarily work for the student. However, if he could instill the right frame of mind into the student, then the rest was up to him. He often confessed to me just how difficult this was, commenting, 'It is easy to teach one to be skillful, but it is difficult to teach him *his own attitude.*'

It was Bruce's considered opinion that the correct attitude towards the martial arts could only be instilled on an individual basis and this is one very important reason why he discarded the idea of setting up a chain of schools. It was part of his talent as a teacher that he needed to get into and open up the minds of his students. What follows here is only one of Bruce's personal routines. It was not designed for his students and he modified this when necessary. As far as his students were concerned he would go to great lengths in order to supply a routine suited to the individual's needs.

1. Sequence training:

sequence 1 (Mon., Wed., Fri.)	sequence 2 (Tues., Thurs., Sat.)
1. Rope jumping	1. Groin stretch
2. Forward bend	2. Side leg raise
3. Cat stretch	3. Jumping squat
4. Jumping jack	4. Shoulder circling
5. Squat	5. Alternate splits
6. High kick	6. Leg stretch—A, B.

2. Forearm/Waist:

sequence 1 (Mon., Wed., Fri.)	sequence 2 (Tues., Thurs., Sat.)
1. Waist twisting	1. Leg raises
2. Palm-up curl	2. Reverse curl
3. Roman chair	3. Sit up twist
4. Knee drawing	4. Leverage bar twist
5. Side bending	5. Alternate leg raise
6. Palm-down curl	6. Wrist roller

3. Power training:

1. Press lockout
2. Press start
3. Rise on toes
4. Pull
5. Squat
6. Shrug
7. Deadlift
8. Quarter squat
9. Frog kick

He also produced an exhaustive course designed to keep pupils fit:

Fitness Program

1. Alternate splits
2. Push up
3. Run in place
4. Shoulder circling
5. High kicks
6. Deep knee bends
7. Side kick raises
8. Sit up twist
9. Waist twisting
10. Leg raises
11. Forward ends

Our home in Bel Air, of course, was filled with special equipment, a great deal of it built for Bruce from his own designs by his friend and student Herb Jackson. Stirling Silliphant expressed himself as appalled by one stretching device which he thought was as tough as a medieval rack. He once wisecracked to Bruce, 'No wonder they talk about Chinese torture.' Another thing that impressed Stirling was a giant bag set up in the garage —a bag four feet wide by five feet high. It required at least two men with outstretched arms to encircle it. This was a soft bag which meant that any kicker had to exert

113

the utmost power to make the slightest impact. 'It was like kicking into a marshmallow,' Stirling says, 'and one heck of a lot bigger than you. And to think that Bruce could send that thing flying with a single kick!' Stirling recalls that Bruce insisted that the greatest thing of all to kick at was a large palm tree. 'He used to tell me, "when you can kick so you aren't jarred, but the tree is jarred, then you will begin to understand a kick." '

Perhaps the one thing about Bruce's death that staggered his fans more than anything else—that makes people as diverse as tribes in Malaya or karate experts and wine salesmen in London refuse to accept that he *is* dead—was the difficulty in crediting that any human being as fit and strong as Bruce could die a natural death at such an early age. One often sees world-class Western boxing champions appearing on TV and admitting that they are 'out of training' or 'not really tuned *up* for a fight'. Bruce, on the other hand, was a fanatic about physical fitness. He never let a day pass without a thorough work-out.

'To me, the best exercise is running,' he once told a reporter, emphasizing that nobody who was not thoroughly fit had 'any business doing any hard sparring'. He insisted that 'running is so important that you should keep it up during your lifetime. What time of the day is not important so long as you run. In the beginning you should jog easily and then gradually increase the distance and tempo, and finally include "sprint" to develop your wind.' He himself ran daily (at least six, sometimes seven days a week) for between fifteen to forty-five minutes, covering from two to six miles. In addition, he covered ten to twenty miles every second day on his stationary bicycle and often went for bicycle rides with Brandon. Besides running, he also believed in exercises for the abdomen—sit-ups, leg-raises and so on: 'Too often one of those big belly Chinese masters will tell you that his *chi* or internal power has sunk to his stomach. He's not kidding, it has sunk—and gone! To put it bluntly, he is nothing but fat and ugly.'

Bruce believed his hands and feet had to be sharpened

and improved daily to be efficient—and indeed, his knuckles were covered with large calluses. Later he discontinued building calluses on his knuckles, feeling that it was only ornamental and could possibly be harmful to the hand's functioning. For example, a bag filled with beans was affixed to a wall and this he used to practice his punching. One unique piece of equipment was a teak dummy which he originally brought from Hong Kong but which he made increasingly sophisticated as he developed his own methods. This piece of equipment was about six feet high and a foot in diameter. It stood upon an eight by eight foot  platform and was supported by springy metal which meant that its reaction to a punch was fairly unpredictable. It had two portable hands below the neck and another in the center which stretched out about two feet. The dummy also had a metal leg which extended out and down. The hands helped in practicing for example *pak sau* (a trapping technique) and also for techniques in *chi sau* (sticking hands). The importance of the dummy foot was that it taught the martial artist to place his foot in such a way as to automatically lock his opponent's leg, thus preventing him from kicking. A student could also practice shin kicks on the dummy.

Bruce, in fact, used several different punching bags.

115

The heavy bag was used to unleash heavy, continuous punches designed to keep an opponent off balance—although the danger was that as it did not react to an attack, it induced a little thoughtlessness on occasions. He used a 'soft bottom' punch bag to hit straight and square. 'If you don't hit it straight, the bag will not return to you,' he explained. It was useful in developing footwork. Supported by springy cords, the bag always returned with enormous speed so that Bruce—or a student—had to be absolutely on the alert. He used a round punching pad with a helper holding it to control height and distance as he struck out towards a moving target. The importance of this was that it taught him not to telegraph punches. It looked something like a baseball mitt, except that it was flat. Bruce actually used to carry one of these things around with him and if he met anyone interested in the martial arts he would take out this mitt, put it on and say 'here, take a swing—all you've got'. Most people would first windup and then hit it. Bruce would ask them to put it on, then show them that it was not necessary to wind up to deliver a punch; all anyone needed was a short distance. He could do this by relaxing and tensing at the right moment—and the severity of the resulting blow was such that on one occasion, he actually dislocated the shoulder of a man in the offices of *Black Belt*.

He even utilized ordinary paper in his workouts. He would hang a sheet of paper on a heavy rope or chain at a chosen height. The purpose of this was to help increase speed and to ensure the correct application of the body for power. It helped develop his hip movement in punching and was also useful for both side and hook kicking. Another derivative of the paper target was that it taught him to judge distance. Its essential purpose. however, was to encourage precision and crisp movement.

Easily one of his most spectacular training movements involved the use of an air shield. This allowed him to develop proper distance and penetration against a moving target, although it could also be used as a static target. This was fascinating to watch. If Bruce held the target for a student. I never saw the student's kick shake him —but inevitably, when it came to Bruce's turn to deliver the kick, the pupil often ended up across the room, stunned. When Bruce's younger brother Robert came to live with us from Hong Kong, he remembers that however hard he tried to brace himself to take one of Bruce's blows at the air s h i e l d , he inevitable ended up on his back in the rear garden—but as h e adds, 'fortunately somebody — probably Linda—always opened the door first'. The shield was also used, of course, to improve penetration. If a partner or pupil thought that Bruce intended to attack, he could try to back away as quickly as possible—though such were Bruce's penetrative powers that even top karatemen found themselves unable to evade him during workouts. Bruce himself emphasized that the best training of all was free-style sparring using protective equipment. 'In sparring you should wear suitable protective equipment and go all out. Then you can truly learn the correct timing and distance for the delivery of kicks, punches, etc. It's a good idea to spar with all types of individuals—tall, short, fast, clumsy —yes, at times a clumsy fellow will mess up a better man because his awkwardness serves as a sort of broken rhythm. The best sparring partner,

though, is a quick, strong man who does not know any-thing, a mad man who goes all out scratching, grabbing, punching, kicking etc.'

This was Bruce's life, then. Up early every day followed by a warm-up of stretching. Perhaps a run before breakfast or a ten-mile jaunt on the stationary bicycle. Then he relaxed by reading, watching some TV, playing with the kids (Brandon had now been joined by our daughter Shannon) or making business calls. An early lunch, followed by more reading—really heavy reading —followed eventually by a rigorous workout. Then before turning in around eleven p.m., he would dictate to his cassette tape-recorder all the matters he needed to attend to the following day. Throughout that whole day, he would have been rarely still. Even while reading, he always had a burlap-covered stool next to him at his desk, pounding away on it with one hand while he turned the pages of his book with the other. He was the nearest thing to perpetual motion in a human being it was possible to imagine.

Then came that disastrous day in 1970, when he damaged his lower back. He was in dreadful pain for more than three months and had to undergo treatment with cortisone. Even then, he found it impossible to remain inactive. He read all the works of Krishnamurti —but unlike most people who might be content to take in the general picture, he underlined key passages or scribbled comments in the margins, all showing that he had found a way of applying some of Krishnamurti's ideas to Jeet Kune Do. Although it was a truly dispiriting time—physical agony compounded by considerable financial worries, it was an experience which, I believe, eventually contributed to his growth. To begin with, for the very first time in years, he had the opportunity to sort out some of the riot of ideas, opinions and philosophies which he had been avidly ingesting for years. Bruce was rarely satisfied just to imbibe ideas, however. He had a tremendous capacity for soaking up knowledge but where he differed from most people was in his insistence on transferring the thought into action.

118

That was the way he l i v e d; transmogrifying thought into action or reversing the process and turning a c t i o n i n t o thought. Even while he spent months of pain-wracked existence, he wrote six whole volumes of material, embracing all his ideas and thoughts, seeking to sort them out into a coherent whole; searching f o r ways of applying ideas to his work.

His back always worried him after that—he was never completely relieved. A lot of men, I believe, would have decided to give up such a strenuous art as kung fu but Bruce, who had a very high threshold of pain and who could

stand a lot—something which he had trained himself to endure—believed that the will could just about overcome anything and finally got to the point where he said he was simply not going to let it stand in his way. He was back to teaching and, apparently, to leading a normal life within six months.

Psychologically, of course, the pressures on him were intense. As his lawyer Adrian Marshall puts it, 'He was still bursting with vitality—he gave you this impression of a man in a terrible hurry.' Perhaps the worst of these was a sense of frustration. He had all these tremendous ideas and tremendous drive and he was so sure he could be an important force in world films—that via the medium of film, he could put across kung fu to the world. On a personality level, everyone agreed that he could make it. 'Bruce, you're great—and you'll be really great when you do a film or something like that,' people would tell him. They probably meant it kindly, but their very faith in him, the knowledge that he was not alone in thinking himself potentially a superstar, intensified his frustrations rather than ameliorated them. The Hollywood movie structure agreed that he was great, had a great personality and charisma and all that, but he lacked everything necessary to secure big finance—he simply did not have enough screen credits. Worse, he was Chinese—and it was difficult to persuade the men who had to put up the money to risk their money on a comparatively unknown Chinese. It is hard to blame them—and Bruce himself never blamed them. He used to explain to me that movies were not an art—'they're a combination of commercial creativity and creative commerce'.

For all his highly-strung nature—his push, his drive, his fierce energy, his determination to break through every barrier—Bruce, on the whole, remained remarkably bright and sunny and even good-tempered. It was less difficult to live with Bruce than even he imagined because it was so obvious that the children and I meant so much to him; that much of what he was trying to achieve was so that he could give us a better life. For most of the time, despite his temperament and the pressures on him, both from within himself and from the frustrations caused by other people, he remained remarkably even-tempered. But he could flare up; he could explode. As his younger brother Robert puts it, 'Sometimes he got in a bad temper—and when I say bad, I mean *bad*. He's not the kind of person who cares who's around—when he's mad, he's mad.' Robert remembers when he and Bruce were attempting to unload a five-hundred-pound crate from a pick-up truck, that Bruce accidentally struck his head on the automatic garage door. The crate had been hard to handle and Robert, who had recently arrived from Hong Kong skinny and relatively weak, had been of little help to

Bruce who, as Robert puts it, 'simply got madder and madder because I was unable to help properly'. That bang on the head was the last straw. In a foul temper Bruce jumped in the truck and started to drive away. Leaving the kids with Robert I hopped in alongside him. We drove around for a few hours and silently brought ourselves together, returning relaxed and pleasant as if nothing had happened.

As Adrian Marshall says, 'I think we've got to see this as all part of the creative and artistic temperament. I mean, I don't think Bruce liked being mad. But it was simply part of his vitality. Mostly, Bruce was  a very courteous man—although he never believed in pulling his punches; he was not going to be fooled or put upon by anybody. And he got away with things that no man who didn't have his charm could never have done. For instance, he could put you down—and you wouldn't feel the slightest degree of offense; he didn't mean to be offensive and unless you were a fool you didn't take it that way. But he did like showing you how good he was. For example, he said to me one day, "Let me see your side-kick"—so I gave the big bag in his house a kick and he said, "Now let me show you what a real side-kick feels like." So he stationed me behind his big bag, then he jumped and the bag hit me in the back. It was like being propelled by a cannon—and I went bang into the wall. But if he put you through it on occasions, he always wanted to help you up again—he wanted you to gain something from the experience. He would say, "Turn the stumbling block into a stepping stone." Whenever something went wrong or you found yourself up against a difficulty, he tried to turn the problem into something of a positive, rather than a negative nature— "This is good, because now you realize that you can overcome that, and I can guarantee you that you will." And nine times out of ten, you did. Mind you, it didn't always work—but it worked for him; but no doubt that was because he had talent.'

Bruce was never petty and rarely petulant. He was not a proud man, but a confident man. Yet trifles could upset him. Adrian Marshall recalls how upset Bruce was when an instructor at a karate studio in Los Angeles actually claimed that he had taught Bruce a certain technique. Bruce flew into a rage about that. He was not annoyed at the idea that people should think there were still tips and techniques that he could learn—he never concealed his debt to Yip Man, for instance; but what really drove him mad was the idea that another man should try to steal the credit for something which he himself had created. 'He got noticeably upset,' recalls Adrian Marshall. 'I must confess it didn't seem all that important to me and yet I can imagine that if it related to my own profession, if I were the innovator of some technique and somebody else tried to grab the credit, I suppose it would probably disturb me too.' The man at the karate studio deeply regretted making the claim. For a long time he lived in fear that Bruce would storm into his *dojo* one day and beat him up. But Bruce had more important matters on his mind than the claims made by rival martial arts instructors.

If the mountain wouldn't come to Mahomet, then he would go to the mountain. He realized that the only way of breaking through the barriers that were preventing him from becoming a huge success in Hollywood was to take a secondary role or a co-starring role in a production associated with the martial arts. Once he was actually *on* the screen; once the wider international public for full-length motion pictures had seen the marvels of gung fu as only he could choreograph them himself, then he would begin to fulfill a major part of his ambitions.

In his mind, the idea for *The Silent Flute* was born.

EIGHT

'In my whole life,' declares Stirling Silliphant, 'no man, no woman, was ever as exciting as Bruce Lee.'

It was natural, of course, that Bruce should seek the help of Stirling and James Coburn when he conceived the idea of a film-story based on the martial arts which was later entitled *The Silent Flute*. Both were his pupils; both had, for a long time, acted as his unofficial advisers with regard to film and TV parts. All three were deeply involved in the martial arts and wanted to do 'the definitive film' on them. In early 1969, they hired a writer to develop a script. This, unfortunately, bore no resemblance to Bruce's original concept and contained none of the ingredients they were all after, so it was turned over to Stirling's nephew, Mark, who also writes screenplays. Again, it didn't work out, so in desperation the three men decided to sit down together and work out the whole thing themselves. It was a labor of love, for they had no guarantee of production. But for the next few months they met three times a week (every Monday, Wednesday and Friday) from four p.m. to six p.m., having pledged each other that they would allow nothing to interfere with that schedule, 'without fail or excuses, above work and family, until it was done'. Stirling then gave the draft script a final polish and sent it to Warner Brothers. The studio liked it—but made the proviso that the film had to be shot in India where they had a large sum of 'blocked rupees' (money their films had earned in India but which the Indian Government refused to remit to the U.S.). India was nobody's idea of the right locale for a Chinese story, but the three men intrepidly set off, hoping for the best. Jim Coburn was to be the 'name' in the film but Bruce, who was to play five different roles, would unquestionably dominate the story. Altogether they spent three weeks in India, trying to find the right place. Jim Coburn thought none of the places was artistically right and, on the whole, didn't enjoy himself all that much; the traveling was very tiring. Bruce created a sensation everywhere he went, of course; he was delighted to 'ham it up', going through some of his kung fu routines and demonstrating some of his party tricks for crowds of youngsters, making coins disappear, and so on.

India, of course, is an old home of the martial arts and Bruce was very keen to see what kind of artists worked there. One day he went out to meet a bunch of

Indian practitioners and he started off by saying, 'Now, let's see where you're at—what you can do?' As Jim Coburn says, 'Then all of a sudden, it was just chaos. There were these nine guys and they just started beating hell out of each other—really boffing each other. So Bruce held up his hand and shouted, "Now, hold it a moment—you're really hurting each other." You know, it was really funny in a way; they had no idea of self-defense—there was actually blood streaming from one guy's mouth. "No, no!" Bruce shouted at them, "Look, this is what I mean." So, without any warm-up, Bruce gave them a little routine demonstration—and they were absolutely awed. They had no conception of this kind of thing. When he'd finished, they all went down on their knees. I mean that.'

The idea, of course, was that if satisfactory locales could be found, some of the Indian martial artists would be used in the film. 'No way,' Bruce told his partners. 'It would take me at least three years to train any of those fellows to the right level.'

Three weeks in the intense heat, with constant traveling and increasing feelings of frustration and a realization that the trip was bound to prove abortive, helped to create a little friction between the three men. Stirling recalls that it was the first time he realized that Bruce was as capable of an ego trip as any other actor. The trouble was that at all the big hotels, James Coburn got the 'star' treatment from the management whereas both Bruce and Stirling had to be content with second-best. One evening, Bruce could no longer contain himself and complained to Stirling that they deserved at least equal treatment. Stirling says it didn't lessen his respect for Bruce; merely made him see him in a more realistic light. Hitherto Bruce had been the *sifu*, the teacher, the philosopher; now here he was declaring impassionately that one day he would be a bigger star than either James Coburn or Steve McQueen.

'I told him there was no way he could be that,' says Stirling. 'That he was a Chinese in a world run by white men. But I was wrong—and how! For in the end he went out and proved himself.'

Silent Flute itself contained many of the themes that reflected Bruce's life and behavior. The script traces a young student's evolution through the martial arts, his problems of ego, his new-found courage in facing the abyss of death, and finally his spiritual rebirth. At one point Bruce says in the script, 'I'm not even sure what trials I passed through—or how I came to be here. I still have doubts, many doubts . . . how, without more struggle, can I resolve them?'

Bruce was very excited at the prospect of doing 'Flute' because he thought it was an idea role for his debut as a major star. He had predicted that kung fu would win world-wide popularity and he believed he was the right man to introduce it to the world through the medium of film. He desperately wanted that film made but when Jim Coburn decided that it was not possible to make a film about kung fu in India, Warner Brothers jettisoned the project. A few years later, by which time Bruce had become a world sensation and offers were pouring in from all sides, Jim and Stirling tried to revive it. Jim actually came out to Hong Kong to talk over the project with Bruce. This time, however, it was Bruce who was in a position to make the vital decisions—and he said no. I think Stirling and Jim were somewhat affronted by Bruce's attitude and even felt that he was snubbing them. After all, it was Bruce who had started the whole project. But by that time—1973—there were too many other pressures on Bruce; everybody wanted him and the role itself would have been a backward step for him. There was never any question of resentment so far as Bruce was concerned. But the situation *had* changed and he believed that Jim and Stirling, as two experienced professionals themselves, would have been the first to recognize that their own decision would have been similar had they been placed in Bruce's circumstances. Certainly

Jim Coburn and Stirling have never lost their admiration and affection for Bruce and Jim was not only among the pallbearers when we laid Bruce to rest in Seattle, but delivered the eulogy.

When Bruce (he took Brandon along with him) made a quick trip home to Hong Kong in 1970 to see his mother and arrange for her to live in America, he was completely stunned by his reception. He had absolutely no idea of how famous he had become in Hong Kong. He simply had not realized that *The Green Hornet* had been one of the most popular TV shows in Hong Kong and throughout Southeast Asia; that he had become a great popular hero. Now he came back to find that every

127

Chinese breast was swollen with pride at the achievement of the home town boy in America. Newspapers demanded interviews, radio men stuck microphones in front of his face; he was invited to appear on Hong Kong's two TV channels. The old films he had made before he left for America were still among the most popular offerings on these channels. As Jim Coburn puts it, 'He was like the King of Hong Kong.' And when he appeared on TV, 'he just about killed everybody'.

He put on a stunning performance for Hong Kong TV. All his bubble and charm and wit came to the surface when he was interviewed. Then he got up and gave a supercharged demonstration of his art. Millions, I believe, gasped. Five one-inch boards were dangled in the air and Bruce just leaped up and side-kicked them and broke four! While the audience were still clapping and howling, Bruce led little Brandon out (he was then five) and he broke some boards, too.

The great reception he received in the city where he was reared undoubtedly played a part in Bruce's eventual decision to return to Hong Kong for good. But, in the meantime, his career still lay in Hollywood. There was the first episode of *Longstreet* to be produced; there were still his well-heeled kung fu clients to be attended to. He was still as choosy as ever about the clients he would accept: In a magazine article he wrote on Jeet Kune Do, he revealed the kind of reasoning that lay behind decisions of this kind. He wrote: 'A teacher does not depend on a method and drill systematic routines; instead, he studies each individual student and awakens him to explore himself, both internally and externally, and ultimately integrating himself with his being. Such teaching, which is really no teaching, requires a sensitive mind with great flexibility and is difficult to come by nowadays.

'Sincere and serious learners are equally difficult to come by. Many of them are five-minute enthusiasts, some of them come with ill intention, but unfortunately, most of them are secondhand artists, basically conformers.' As Adrian Marshall puts it. 'Bruce didn't accept pupils just because they were famous—or because they could pay the big fees demanded. He was only interested in teaching serious artists —he didn't want to be used as a kind of clown, I think.'

But events were suddenly speeding up for Bruce— events that were to snatch him away from teaching altogether and whirl him up into the d i z z y stratosphere of superstardom. The first episode of *Longstreet*. Bruce's 'Way of the Intercepting Fist' hit American screens with sizzling impact. It was so good that producers of the show decided to open their autumn schedules with i.t—t h a t highly competitive time of the year when, as the nights begin to close in and summer fades, viewers flock around their small screens, hungry for entertainment. Bruce, by virtue of Stirling's subtle script, had an opportunity not only to demonstrate the lethal effectiveness of kung fu but was able to get across some of the philosophical notions that lay behind his art. For instance, when James Franciscus, the blind insurance detective, asks Bruce to teach him kung fu, Bruce replied 'I cannot teach you, I can only help you explore yourself.' Later on, he tells Longstreet, 'You must learn defeat— like most people you want to learn to win.'

The reviews in the trade press and the big newspapers such as the New York *Times* and the Los Angeles *Times* were, almost without exception, excellent. They were very different in kind from anything Bruce had ever earned as Kato. His kung fu techniques had been acclaimed as something fresh and startling, but Bruce the actor had been largely ignored. This time, the accent was on Bruce's talents as an actor. It pleased him immensely: 'It was the first time in my life I had *any* kind of review for my acting,' he told *Fighting Stars* magazine.

One of the misconceptions about Bruce, of course, is that he could not help becoming a success because he was blessed with such considerable natural talent. Of course, he had talent; but it has always seemed to me that not enough attention has been paid to how hard Bruce worked to improve and perfect all his abilities. He trained harder as a kung fu expert than any man I have ever known or heard about; he flung himself into the task of acting with a concentration that only a man who burned up energy like a furnace could achieve. Talent is supposed to find its own outlets; create its own opportunities; like murder, it is supposed to 'out'. But in Bruce's case it seemed to me that intense desire—for, above all, Bruce was driven by intense desire—created not only its own opportunities but its own talents.

While he was busy on *Longstreet,* an irresistible demand for his services had begun up in the Orient. 'After I left Hong Kong,' Bruce revealed to *Fighting Stars* magazine, 'the media there kept in contact with me by telephone. Those guys used to call me early in the morning and even kept a conversation going on the air, so the public was listening to me. Then one day, the announcer asked me if I would do a movie there. When I replied that I would do it if the price was right, I began to get calls from producers in Hong Kong and Taiwan. Offers to do a movie varied from two thousand U.S. dollars to ten thousand.'

Things were moving fast now. Bruce's fan mail after the *Longstreet* episode was considerably more than that of the star's, James Franciscus. Hollywood studios and producers really began to sit up and take notice. Even

130

before this, Warner Brothers had suddenly caught on to the fact that kung fu itself had captured the public's imagination and decided to launch a TV series. Bruce himself had been working on the idea of a Shaolin priest, a master of kung fu, who would roam America and find himself involved in various exploits. The studio contacted him and he was soon deeply involved. He gave them numerous ideas, many of which were eventually incorporated in the resulting TV success, *Kung Fu*, starring actor David Carradine.

On the whole, Bruce was to suffer a severe rebuff over this series. He had mixed feelings to begin with. He had long talks with Jim Coburn who advised him: 'Man, you go into TV and you're going to burn out your show in a season. Television chews up genius—it can chew a man up in a series of thirteen episodes; it's a waste of time. Set your sights on Hong Kong, instead.' Bruce used to come home and tell me what Jim had said—that TV was too short-lived; that he ought to consider Hong Kong where he could be more specific. All the same, the idea of a nationwide series was unquestionably attractive and he would, almost certainly, have liked to have done it very much. But in the end, of course, he was glad he had not done it. But the shattering fact was that Warner Brothers never offered it to him. I understand that

neither Warner Brothers or ABC had even considered starring Bruce in the series; they thought he was too small; too Chinese; that he wasn't a big enough name to sustain a weekly series; that he was too inexperienced. I doubt if they ever really tried to rationalize their ideas; they obviously just didn't see him as the right heavyweight material. Probably it just never occurred to them that a Chinese could become a hero in a white man's world; even Stirling Silliphant, for all his awe and respect for Bruce, had instinctively felt the same way.

Through a friend in Hong Kong, Bruce heard that a film offer from Run Run Shaw, the Chinese millionaire who almost single-handedly had founded the highly (commercially speaking) successful Hong Kong film industry and owns a chain of cinemas throughout southeast Asia, was on its way. The offer finally came through —and for all the rumors of offers and approaches it was, in fact, the first solid offer Bruce had received. Bruce laughed it off—Run Run's offer was two thousand U.S. dollars a film and he knew Shaw would expect to sign him on a long-term contract (normally he hired actors and actresses on a six-year contract and churned out his films for less than £40,000). At one stage, Bruce did go so far as to wire Shaw asking about script details and other matters. Shaw's reply was a paternalistic, 'Just tell him to come back here and everything will be all right.' This was rubbing Bruce up the wrong way with a vengeance.

For all this, and despite his irritations with the Hollywood movie structure, Bruce still thought his future lay in America and he had no real desire to return to Hong Kong either to work or live. Then, out of the blue, came the kind of chance he had been looking for. Raymond Chow, who had been a producer and director with Run Run Shaw's outfit for many years had, in 1970, decided to launch out on his own and had formed Golden Harvest Productions. It was a move which led to bitter rivalry and enmity between Shaw and Chow; an antipathy exacerbated when Raymond Chow made a determined approach to Bruce. Throughout his time in Hong Kong Bruce repeatedly made it clear that he was not interested in local film politics. He was on nobody's side in the fight between Run Run Shaw and Golden Harvest or other independent producers; he was primarily concerned with his own interests. With considerable acumen Raymond Chow dispatched one of his senior producers to interview Bruce in Hollywood. This was Mrs. Lo Wei, wife of one of his top directors. The money itself was not all that wonderful; seventy-five hundred dollars per film. Not all that wonderful by Hollywood standards, perhaps, but good by Hong Kong standards. But there was to be no long-term contract nonsense—the contract was for two films only. Before actually signing the contract. Bruce prepared by going to see 'a whole bunch of Mandarin movies'. As he said later, 'They were awful. For one thing, everybody fights all the time, and what really bothered me was that they all fought exactly the same way. Wow, nobody's really like that. When you get into a fight, everybody reacts differently, and it is possible to act and fight at the same time. Most Chinese films have been very superficial and one dimensional.'

There was some further 'politicking' necessary before Bruce was prepared to put his actual signature to the contract. Run Run Shaw was still in there fighting for Bruce's services so Raymond Chow decided that rather than allow Bruce to set foot in Hong Kong where he might be snatched from under his nose, that the star capture should fly direct to Bangkok where the film was to be shot. Bruce refused; he was determined to stamp his authority on his productions from the outset insofar as was reasonable. It was not a question of ego; it was a question of making it clear from the outset that he was his own man. So in July 1971, Bruce landed in Hong Kong. He stayed at the airport only long enough to greet a friend and to show that he was not going to be moved around like a pawn, then he flew on to Bangkok.

Shortly after he had actually appended his signature to the contract, a Taiwan producer telephoned him. 'The

135

guy told me to rip up the contract and he'd top Raymond's offer and even take care of any lawsuit for breaking the agreement', Bruce later told a magazine. Such men had little concept of Bruce's character and intelligence. Once he had signed his name, that was that. Besides which, he had almost a sixth sense, as his lawyer Adrian Marshall confirms, about offers, the kind of men who made them and the degree of say and authority he might be able to exert. He knew he could persuade Raymond Chow to go along with most of his ideas, the first of which was to persuade the producer to make a martial arts film with only the minimum use of weapons. Until then, most Chinese movies had tried to emulate the Japanese samurai (warrior) movies and the use of words and other weapons had been heavily emphasized.

On a hot and humid day in July then, Bruce found himself dumped down in the little village of Pak Chong, north of Bangkok. It was rural, primitive and cut off to a degree beyond belief; the very last place on earth, one would have thought, from which to start one of the most legendary careers in the history of motion pictures. It was here that Bruce physically met Raymond Chow for the first time. The two men shook hands and afterwards were able to laugh at Bruce's first words. With sublime assurance and confidence, he declared, 'You just wait, I'm going to be the biggest Chinese star in the world.'

Within months, he had proved to be right. Like a brief, bright meteor he was suddenly to blaze and flare with an intensity of light that would eclipse anything emitted by any other star in the motion picture heavens.

NINE

That first letter from Bruce in Pak Chong revealed the whole awful picture: 'Bangkok was fine. However, Pak Chong is something else. The mosquitoes are terrible and cockroaches are all over the place. The main reason for not having written is for lack of services, but also, had a rather nasty accident— as I was washing up a superthin glass, my grip broke the damn thing and cut my right hand rather deep—the worst cut I have, that requires ten stitches. Don't worry, though, I am sure within two or three weeks I will be okay, though it is inconvenient for me to write (or take a bath or anything, for the past week).

'I have got to find out the confirmation of you people coming—though I a mpretty damn sure. They want me to do a short film on JKD [Jeet Kune Do] in exchange for your fare. I'm in no condition to do it but I'm sure they won't want to press matters because since my arrival, everyone, including the Shaw Brothers are calling and using all means to get me. One thing is for sure, I'm the super star in H.K. . . . I'm writing rather poorly due to my hand—it's much better now. I'm taking my vitamin pills and though I'm down to 128 I'm getting used to the conditions here—the cockroaches are a constant threat, the lizards I can ignore—I just want you to know I miss all of you and am sending my love to you all . . . take care my love. Love and kisses . . .'

There were all sorts of troubles: 'Another director (a fame lover) just arrived supposedly to take over the present director's job. It really doesn't matter, as long as he is capable as well as co-operative. . . . The food is terrible, this village has no beef and very little chicken and pork. Am I glad I came with my vitamins. I wish you were here because I miss you and the children a lot. This village is terrible. No place like home. I'm looking forward to meeting you in Hong Kong. . . . My personal love to my wife . . . and Brandon, Shannon.'

Only July 28, he wrote: 'It's been 15 days since my arrival in Pak Chong and it seems already like a year! Due to lack of meat, I have to get canned-meat for lunch. I'm glad to have brought along the vitamins.

'I miss you a lot but Pak Chong is *no* place for you and the children. It's an absolute underdeveloped village and a big nothing.

'The film I'm doing is quite amateur-like. A new director has replaced the uncertain old one; this new director is another so-so one with an almost unbearable air of superiority.

'At any rate, I'm looking forward to leaving Pak

Bruce in training doing arm-forward pushups

Chong for Bangkok where it is at least halfway decent. Then I'll fly to Hong Kong and make the necessary arrangements for you people to come over—looking forward to seeing the three of you very much indeed.

'My voice is gone (very hoarse!!) from yelling and talking under really terrible conditions—machine running, ice cutting etc, etc. Anyway, all hell broke loose here. My back is getting along fair—need lots of rest after a fight scene.

'Have to go and eat now—see if I can find any meat. Love to you my dearest wife. With kisses.'

Another letter: 'Haven't heard from Paramount— maybe Sept. is a little bit too late for returning for *Longstreet*—time will tell. Can you send some pictures of you and the children?

'The future looks extremely bright indeed, with lots

. . . but on his thumbs only!

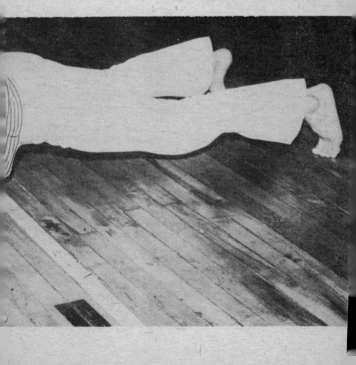

of possibilities ahead—big possibilities. Like the song says, "We've only just begun".

'I have a feeling Stirling won't be able to finish the script in time for me to come back in Sept. At any rate one way or other I really don't mind too much, the Lee family is enjoying some nice moments ahead. My love to you my dearest.'

Another:

'Linda,

'To make sure of arriving the States on time, I've gone through two days of hell. I sprained my ankle rather badly from a high jump on a slipped mattress—which required a drive of two hours to Bangkok to see a doctor—consequently I caught the flu (Bangkok is hot and stuffy and the traffic is a 24 hours jam). Anyway, with fever, cold aches and pain, we used close ups while I dragged my leg to finish the last fight.

'I feel all right now except for my ankle and am doing well in Bangkok . . . I can tell you one thing, things are happening too damned fast here.

'Well, at least at Thai Hotel I have breakfast in bed, nothing like Pak Chong. By the way I picked up a his and her "something" for both of us. It's a surprise for our anniversary. You will have to wait for me to bring them to you.

'Happy anniversary, my sweet wife!'

Enclosed was a short note for Brandon, printed out in capital letters:

'Hello Brandon! When I come back we will go to the toy shop. Love you my son.

Dad

'P.S. Will you kiss Ma Ma and Shannon for me?'

Again:

'Linda,

'I'm writing this letter to let you know that

A) *Longstreet* is such a success that reaction is instantaneous whenever my character comes up.

B) So Paramount is asking me to re-appear and stay as a recurrent character.

C) So that means I might get a one month leave after

140

Sept. 1 and fly back to finish three more shows or whatever and then fly to Hong Kong with you and the kids to finish the second picture.

D) Of course, that means killing two birds with one stone and getting extra bread.

E) I've already wired Tannenbaum for him to let me know of his "arrangements" for me.

'My dearest wife,

'Today, I've sent the telegram. However, it won't be till Monday Tannenbaum will receive it, unless there is extra service in the studio during the weekend.

'Anyway, what it amounts to is a few more days of wondering how it will turn out. Disregard the consequences. I am firm on my ground of "it's about time to raise my worth". Well, it's a matter of whether I'm coming back to meet you and then fly together to Hong Kong or you and the kids flying over to meet me in Hong Kong. I have to say the first choice is more profitable and full of possibility. Time will tell.

'Though I have to say the house-payment troubles me somewhat I'm sure you will find the best possible way out. I hate to have an overall change of payment.

'Anyway, my future in acting has now begun. I'm sure the one I'm doing now will be a big success—again, time will tell. Though the place I'm in is rather hell, I'm in the profession where I belong and love to do.

'Take care my love. It won't be long for us to get together'

'Linda,

'By now, you should have received my letter regarding hoping to extend the loan or the best way, whatever it might be.

'Received telegram from Paramount extracted as follows:

"freelance offer for not less than three episodes at one thousand per episode. Each episode, not to take more than three days from Sept. 5 to Sept. 30th—1st class round trip ticket—imperative we hear from you immediately to prepare script for the character you portray."

'Well, here is my answer:
"My usual two thousand per episode plus quality technical advising. If acceptable can start work from Sept. 7 to Oct. 7. Notify immediately for schedule arrangement."

'Really, if Paramount *really* likes me and if I really did such a good job, I feel I should advance to at least two grand per episode, disregard three days or anything. Let's face it. My billing isn't exactly there. Who knows what the future holds? I feel rather definite about this, don't you?

'There comes a time when you have to advance or retreat—this time I can always retreat to my Hong Kong deal. . . .'

These had been extraordinary weeks for both of us. I

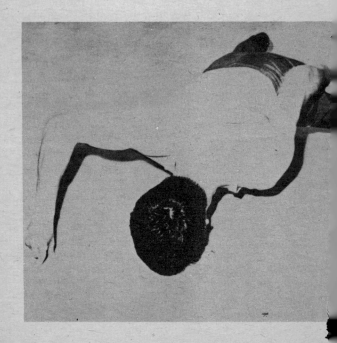

had found myself involved in all the excitement as the desperate Paramount executives, unable to trace Bruce by telephone or cable, sought me as an intermediary. Once that first episode of *Longstreet* had appeared, all the world, it seemed, suddenly wanted to get hold of Bruce. First it was Run Run Shaw, then independent producers, finally Paramount. 'They couldn't get me because I really was in the sticks,' Bruce explained to reporters later. 'It's funny, but when Paramount sent telegrams and telephoned Hong Kong for me, boy, the producers thought I was an important star. My prestige must have increased three times.'

Finally, he clinched the deal with Paramount and returned to Hollywood to play in three more episodes of *Longstreet*. The difficulty was that these three episodes had been planned before 'The Way of the Intercepting Fist' appeared. Faced with Bruce's success, Stirling Silliphant was asked to somehow work him into the fresh episodes; in the event, even Stirling could do little more

One-handed finger-and-thumb pushup. Bruce's physical fitness was superb.

than create walk-through parts for him. That first episode had been one of the finest showcases Bruce could have hoped for; his role in the succeeding episodes, therefore, seemed to him a sort of anti-climax.

Yet whatever Bruce's feelings, the significant thing was that the Hollywood movie structure had seen the light. Both Paramount and Warner Brothers (the same people who had first raised his hopes about the *Kung Fu* TV series and had then so abruptly dashed them) rushed in with option offers. In October 1971, Warner Brothers made him the following proposal:

1. 25,000 (U.S. dollars) for which WB to receive an exclusive hold on his TV services in order to develop a project for him.
2. If we go to pilot, the following fees would be applicable against the 25,000 dollars.
   a. Half-hour pilot—10,000
   b. One hour pilot—12,500
   c. Ninety-minute pilot—15,000
   d. Two hour pilot—17,500.

If for any reason we did not make a pilot, it might be a good idea to apply the 25,000 towards a feature deal.

3. SERIES PRICES
   a. Half-hour—3,000 per original telecast—scale residuals.
   b. One-hour—4,000 per original telecast—scale residuals.

The offers were not only flattering—but inviting. It was at this time that Bruce, certain that he stood on the threshold of great success, consulted Jim Coburn; that Jim repeated his advice about TV 'chewing up geniuses' and that Bruce should pin his hopes on Hong Kong instead. In the light of the stupendous success of *The Big Boss* (released through most of the world as *Fists of Fury*) it would seem to have been an easy decision. But the fact was that although that landmark in films was in the can by then, it had yet to be premiered. Bruce, in-

144

deed, although he had seen the rushes, had never seen the film stitched together and edited. He had no idea what reaction it might draw—although he knew he had done well. Remember that films about the martial arts had been a staple of Hong Kong movies for years in much the same way as Westerns in America. A report in the Los Angeles *Times* in January 1973 explains the situation: 'The simple message is that violence is apparently more appealing than the convoluted sexual and psychological intricacies of the West,' a screenwriter observed.

'And let's keep it that way,' a visiting distributor from Caracas added, 'I'm afraid the new karate and boxing films are getting too complicated for my customers. They like the good old simple sword fighting films.

'Basically,' the scriptwriter said, 'almost every really successful Mandarin movie of the past decade comes down to one theme—revenge. For good reason, we Chinese today are obsessed with revenge. . . . Confucius himself warned against the passion 2,500 years ago. . . . But Raymond Chow feels that the new emphasis on unarmed combat, rather than sword play, will enable him to satisfy both bloodthirsty audiences and the censors.'

Bruce had not really reached any firm decisions when he returned to Hong Kong. His contract with Raymond Chow called for a second film, *Fists of Fury*. His intentions were, vaguely, to finish his two films for Chow, then return to Hollywood and take up some of his TV offers. Everything, however, got blown away one wonderful night in October 1971 when we attended the midnight premiere of *The Big Boss* in Hong Kong. Every dream that Bruce had ever possessed came true that night. The audience rose to its feet, yelling, clapping, cheering. It was almost impossible to leave the theater; we were absolutely mobbed. In less than two hours of action on the screen, Bruce became a glittering star. One American entertainment editor wrote: 'That film is the finest acting job of Bruce Lee's career. It is one of the most outstanding examples of sheer animal presence on celluloid ever produced. I would match it against the best of Clint Eastwood, Steve McQueen or the various James Bonds.'

The plot, by Western tastes, was relatively simple; indeed, brutally naïve. It centers around the struggles of a group of Chinese in Bangkok who are terrorized by gangsters involved in drugs. Bruce finds himself working in an ice factory which is really a front for the mob. For most of the film, Bruce suffers insults and indignities because he has made a promise to his family to reform after years of giving them trouble. His efforts to hold back his temper, his eyes actually *bulge* with the effort, have the audiences sitting on the edges of their seats with tension. Finally, when the sheer pitch of frustration becomes well-nigh unbearable, Bruce cuts loose. 'What happens then is amazing to say the least,' wrote one critic, 'he systematically wipes out the opposition in a series of incredible fights. There is one fight which you'll remember for a long time to come, fighting one of the groups of Mi's henchmen, he puts one of the men against the wall and with an amazing thrust of brute power he knocks the man clean through the wall, leaving the shape of the man in the empty wall.'

Within three weeks, the take at the box office was ahead of the previous record-breaker, *The Sound of Music,* which had grossed 2.3 million Hong Kong dollars inside nine weeks. In fact, *Boss* took over 3.5 million dollars alone in Hong Kong within nineteen days. Then it proceeded to smash all known records throughout the Mandarin circuit and in cities as far away as Rome, Beirut and Buenos Aires. Everything that Bruce had ever hoped for, everything he had said he would do —all was accomplished or on the verge of being so. 'We knew from the outset that the film was going to be a success,' Bruce told reporters, 'but I have to admit we weren't really expecting it to be *that* successful.' He explained that he hoped the film would 'represent a new trend in Mandarin cinema. I mean people *like* films that are more than just one long armed hassle. With any luck, I hope to make multi-level films here—

the kind of movies where you can just watch the surface story if you like, or can look deeper into it. Most of the Chinese films to date have been very superficial and one dimensional. I tried to do that in *The Big Boss*. The character I played was a very simple, straightforward guy. Like, if you told this guy something, he'd believe you. Then, when he finally figures out he's been had, he goes animal. This isn't a bad character, but I don't want to play him all the time. I'd prefer somebody with a little more depth.'

One result of Bruce's success was that *I* found myself being interviewed by newspapers and magazines. I was asked the inevitable question: 'How did I feel when I saw my husband on the screen in the arms of another woman? I could only answer, 'It's difficult to feel romantic when you know you are in front of a camera and under the blaze of powerful lights. It's only part of his job as an actor.' Then I remembered a moment when we had sat in the dark watching *The Big Boss* unfold and the scene comes up where Bruce is brought face to face with a naked prostitute; Bruce had leaned across to me and whispered, 'Part of the fringe benefits.'

One newspaper in the Orient hailed Bruce as the first mid-Pacific man. At the time of the interview Bruce was still toying with the idea of a Hollywood TV series called *The Warrior*. 'What's holding things up now is that a lot of people are sitting around in Hollywood trying to decide if the American television audience is ready for an Oriental hero. We could get some really peculiar reactions from places like the Deep South,' he said. Bruce also told the reporter that he was a little worried that Oriental audiences, on the other hand, might think he was too Western, and admitted there were some scenes where he thought he hadn't been Chinese enough. He revealed much that the cold-blooded men of business, who considered Mandarin movies mere groceries to be packaged up and shoved across the counter to the customers willy-nilly, found almost revolutionary: 'He even worries about arcane things like the artistic progress of the Mandarin cinema,'

147

wrote the reporter, Jack Moore, 'which, he says, will only be possible when local directors get off their individual ego trips and studios start paying better money for better quality.' He explained that he thought his own contribution would be not to make films whose quality was doubtful. 'Everything is overplayed in Mandarin films. To make really good ones, you'd have to use subtlety, and very few people in the business want to risk any money by trying that. On top of which, the scripts are pretty terrible. You wouldn't *believe* all the stuff I re-wrote for *The Big Boss*. All of us have to come secondary to the quality of the film itself.' As Jack Moore wrote: 'Which has to be the most encouraging thing we've heard about Mandarin films for a long time.'

It was revolutionary talk for Hong Kong. And there was a lot more to come, in due course, from the same source.

One consequence of his filming experiences—the humidity, the heat, the constant outpouring of nervous and physical energy—was that Bruce began to lose weight.

To some, Bruce's food intake might seem adequate; but he burned energy like a furnace. Even as a child in Hong Kong, Robert remembers, Bruce was a 'muncher'. 'He'd munch on anything. He'd use his lunch money on candy, his allowance on snacks.' Outside school lurked a corps of vendors peddling all kinds of food—raw squid, octopus and pig intestines which Bruce would 'eat up like candy'.

Even in Los Angeles he had developed an interest in health foods and high protein drinks. Several times a day he took a high protein drink made up of powdered milk, ice water, eggs, eggshells, bananas, vegetable oil, peanut flour, chocolate ice cream—it was more like a thick, unstirrable soup than anything else. He also drank a lot of his own juice concoction made from vegetables and fruits—apples, celery, carrots and so on, prepared in an electric blender. He also drank a lot of honey tea and fresh orange juice in Hong Kong because he perspired so much, particularly while working. He topped

148

these off with Chinese tonics. We bought a lot of our stuff at health stores although it is not true that he refused to eat anything unless it came from one of these. He loved meat and Chinese food, in particular. He liked spicy, hot kimchee and I particularly remember our going to Korean restaurants in Hong Kong with Jhoon Rhee and Bruce would sit there and eat and eat, and sweat and sweat and eat and eat—and he just loved it. He took every possible vitamin pill and in time became very knowledgeable about vitamins and very aware of the dangers and never took more than necessary—making sure that he had the right quota of A, B, C, D, and E. He had the Chinese passion for rice—but he couldn't boil water and I would make it for him; when I say that, I mean he could not cook. For instance, on one occasion when I was away for a day or so, he existed on nothing but marshmallows. In Hong Kong, he also developed a passion for Shredded Wheat. He often used to waken me up at two o'clock in the morning and ask me to go downstairs and prepare him a bowl of Shredded Wheat.

He had been hooked on special food kicks long before he found himself becoming dehydrated in Hong Kong. As Jim Coburn says, 'The thing that really scared me was when he was drinking beef blood—he'd put hamburger in the concoction.' Jim adds, 'That's really bad for your blood.' However, he discontinued this practice before long as he was concerned about the sterility of beef blood. Following Bruce's example, James used to prepare his own high protein drinks until he found he had gout. 'I was taking super high potency protein and my body just couldn't digest them all—I was crippling around and I didn't know what it was, I thought it was arthritis.' In fact, Bruce once found he had a high iodine thyroid count. The doctor couldn't figure out what was causing it and asked him what he had been eating. It turned out that the high iodine count was caused by overindulgence in Japanese seaweed wrapped around rice, and he was ordered to cut out this overindulgence. Throughout our time in Hong

149

Kong, Bruce fought a running battle between his enormous output of energy and his resulting loss of weight.

Meanwhile, his career continued to zoom and a publicity handout had him declaring, 'These films should do for me what the spaghetti westerns did for Clint Eastwood.' Bruce recalled for reporters the tremendous reaction of the audience to his second film called *Fists of Fury*. With Bobby Baker from California, who had a part in the film, Bruce took his place in the balcony seats unnoticed. 'As the movie progressed, we kept looking at the reactions of the fans. They hardly made any noise in the beginning, but at the end they were in a frenzy and began clapping and clamoring. Those fans there are emotional. If they don't like the movie, they'll cuss and walk out. When the movie came to an end, Bob, almost in tears, shook my hand and said, "Boy, am I happy for you!"'

The film was destined to break records everywhere—even those established by *The Big Boss*. Within thirteen days, it had topped *Big Boss*'s record of 3.5 million HK dollars and zoomed towards the four million mark. Not all the critics took a kindly view of it. *South China Morning Post* (Hong Kong) in particular, criticized the handling of the film by the director Lo Wei but claimed that when Bruce 'lashed out, he does it beautifully. The fierce fighting in fits of blind anger is frightening—and superb.' In fact, Bruce himself had become violently disenchanted with Lo Wei during the making of the film and their 'feud' was well-publicized at the time. Bruce's only concern was to make a good film and he was genuinely annoyed that there was no proper script and that production techniques were almost chaotic. He thought Lo Wei didn't seem to be interested in what was going on and at one stage was actually discovered listening to a blaring radio when the actors were supposed to be playing out a romantic love scene.

And yet the success of the film was never in doubt because on at least two levels it delighted Chinese audiences in particular. Bruce was, if anything, more lethal than in *The Big Boss*; more dramatic, more blood-curdling. His kiai or fighting yell—like an angry leopard or panther—came screeching off the screen in a blood-chilling way. His kicks and leaps were more dramatic than ever. He also employed the nunchuks for the first time with deadly effect. He used these vicious truncheons 'with horrific accuracy and bravado' reported one critic. He also knew how to raise a laugh by making fools of his enemies—'he's an actor with a sense of the absurd' noted the same critic admiringly. Yet paradoxically, it was the very plot itself, for all its inadequacies, that made Bruce a hero to millions of Chinese. It appealed to their chauvinism and desire for self-respect in a way that is almost inexplicable to the inhabitants of success-ful Western countries who have never been exploited.

The film opens with the death of the teacher of a Chinese martial arts school in Shanghai around 1908. At the funeral representatives from a Japanese martial arts school present a tablet to *The Sick Man of Asia*. Bruce not only resents the insult but, believing the Japanese were responsible for the teacher's death, decides to avenge his honor. He single-handedly goes to the Japa-nese club and beats up the entire membership. The Japanese retaliate, with the help of a Russian mercenary. In the end, Bruce challenges the top Japanese expert and knocks the stuffing out of both him and the giant Russian. When at one stage, Bruce roars defiantly, 'Chi-nese are not sick men!', audiences erupted from their seats. As a film it was all action and violence. The Chinese are a violent people and Bruce himself was con-cerned with this aspect: 'The glorification of violence is bad. That is why I insisted that the character I played in this film died at the end. He had killed many people and had to pay for it.' Chinese audiences hated his death and many protested, outraged that their hero should be punished.

Bruce himself made clear his attitude in an interview with the *Hong Kong Standard*. He explained, 'I'm dis-satisfied with the expression of the cinematic art here in Hong Kong. It's time somebody did something about the films here. There are simply not enough soulful characters here who are committed, dedicated, and are at the same time professionals. I believe I have a role. The audience needs to be educated and the one to educate them has to be somebody who is responsible. We are dealing with the masses and we have to create something that will get through to them. We have to educate them step by step. We can't do it overnight. That's what I'm doing right now. Whether I succeed or not remains to

from "*Enter The Dragon.*" (Warner Bros.)

be seen. But I just don't *feel* committed, I *am* committed.' He argued that with regard to violence—'I didn't create this monster—all this gore in the Mandarin films. It was there before I came. At least I don't spread violence. I don't call the fighting in my films violence. I call it action. An action film borders somewhere between reality and fantasy. If it were completely realistic, you would call me a bloody violent man. I would simply destroy my opponent by tearing him part or ripping his guts out. I wouldn't do it so artistically. I have this intensity in me that the audience believes in what I do because I do believe in what I do. But I act in such a way as to border my action somewthere between reality and fantasy.' In that same interview he revealed that he would like to evolve in different roles but thought it would be impossible in southeast Asia—that he had become too typecast. 'Besides, I can't even express myself fully on film here, or the audiences wouldn't understand what I am talking about half the time. That's why I can't stay in Southeast Asia all the time. I am improving and making new discoveries every day. If you don't, you are already crystallized and that's it'—and Bruce made a slashing gesture across his throat. 'I'll be doing different types of films in the future, some serious, some philosophical and some pure entertainment. But I will never prostitute myself in any way.'

It was certainly Bruce up there on the screen—but that almost wild animal destroying men like a one-man army was far from being the whole of him. He was simply the dazzling "Three Kick Bruce" to the Chinese world—and every young man in Hong Kong wanted to emulate him and every young girl, if not to marry him, at least be photographed with him. He found his loss of privacy annoying—although he accepted it philosophically enough as the price to be paid for his position.

'The biggest disadvantage', he admitted to *Black Belt* after his first three films had broken records everywhere and had begun penetrating the West, 'is losing your privacy. It's ironic but we all strive to become wealthy and famous, but once you're there, it's not all rosy.

There's hardly a place in Hong Kong where I can go to without being stared at or people asking me for autographs. That's one reason I spend a lot of time at my house to do my work. Right now, my home and the office are the most peaceful places.' He explained that he avoided social gatherings wherever possible (he had never liked them, in fact, even before he became famous): 'I'm not that kind of cat. I don't drink or smoke and those events are many times senseless. I don't like to wear stuffy clothes [he bought himself beautiful shirts and suits—he enjoyed *buying* them—yet he was voted Worst-Dressed Actor of the Year, merely because he liked wearing casual clothes instead] and be at places where everyone is trying to impress each other. Now, I'm not saying I'm modest. I rather like to be around a few friends and talk informally about such things as boxing and the martial arts. Whenever I go to such places as a restaurant, I try to sneak in without being detected. I'll go directly to a corner table and quickly sit down, facing the wall so my back is to the crowd. I keep my head low while eating. No, I'm not crazy. I only look like it. You see, if I'm recognized I'm dead, because I can't eat with the hand that I have to use to sign autographs. And I'm not one of those guys that can brush people off.' Once, in fact, an usherette flashed a torch in his face in the darkness of a cinema and demanded his autograph. 'Now I understand why stars like Steve [McQueen] avoid public places. In the beginning I didn't mind the publicity I was getting. But soon, it got to be a headache answering the same questions over and over again, posing for photos and forcing a smile.' It became worse than just that, actually; time after time, we had to dash crazily from a restaurant to get into our car to avoid being engulfed by a rapturous mob; and then there were the inevitable young punks who wanted to 'prove' to Bruce that they were better than he was.

There was even an influx of martial artists into Hong Kong, hoping to duplicate Bruce's 'luck'. He exploded. 'They think they can be lucky, too. Well, I don't believe in pure luck. You have to create your own luck. You have to be aware of the opportunities around you and take advantage of them. Some guys may not believe it, but I spent hours perfecting whatever I did.'

Explaining that he wanted to be 'The Best Martial Artist', he emphasized that his daily minimum training time was two hours; that this included running three miles as well as stretching and kicking, and hitting his various punching bags. Every afternoon he went 'jogging' in Hong Kong disguising himself as best he could and keeping his head down to avoid being recognized.

Yes, there were undoubtedly the nice things. The red Porsche he had in California gave way to a luxurious Mercedes 350 SL (he drove both cars with the panache —and much of the daring—of Steve McQueen) and he had a gold Rolls-Royce Corniche on order by the time he made his fourth and final film. He always admitted to a passion for cars yet his greatest passion really was for books—but he refused to regard books as material possessions and, instead, saw them as the repositories of ideas, philosophies and religious principles (not that he believed in God—he once wisecracked to his brother Robert when he asked him about God, 'I believe in sleeping'). He liked clothes and enjoyed buying them (but he had never wasted money on them when times had been lean). Both he and I took pleasure in seeing his photographs in all the newspapers and on the front covers of magazines all over the world. Yet in the end, I cannot say it would have worried him much if they hadn't been there.

I prefer to think of him sitting in his study lost in the world of books and ideas. Patiently sketching his beautiful drawings of Taoist priests or wild fighting martial artists from ancient China. Writing or translating expressive poems:

Rain
Black clouds,
Fallen blossoms and pale moon,
The hurried flight of birds,

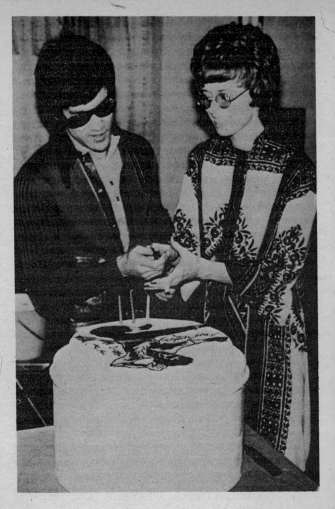

Bruce and Linda Lee celebrate a
happy wedding anniversary.

The arrival of lonely autumn,
The time for us to part.
Much has been said, yet
We have not come to the end of our feeling.
I leave you this poem
Read it where the silence of the world possesses you,
Or when you're fretted with disquiet,
Long must be this parting, and
Remember,
That all my thoughts have always been of you.

I think of Bruce as a man who loved to watch soft, light rain falling; who loved the feel of its touch on his face.

The real Bruce, too, was the man who could sit meditatively and jot down his reflections thus:

'I am learning to understand rather than immediately judge or to be judged. I cannot blindly follow the crowd and accept their approach.'

or:

'Ever since I was a kid, the word "quality" has meant a geat deal to me. The greatest satisfaction is to hear another unbiased human being whose heart has been touched and honestly says, "Hey, here is some-one real!" I'd like that! In life, what can you ask for but to be real, to fulfill one's mission and above all actualize one's potential instead of dissipating one's image, which is not real and expending one's vital energy. We have great work ahead of us and it needs devotion and much, much energy. To grow, to discover, we need involvement, which is something I experience every day, sometimes good, sometimes frustrating. No matter what, you let your inner light guide you out of the darkness.

'For those who want to know, I am a martial artist by choice, an actor by profession (which to me is an expressive revelation and/or learning of myself) and am actualizing myself daily to be an artist of life as well. After all, all arts have a similar foundation: one's

157

choice of freedom in expressing one's instinctive potentialities.'

And:

'I will not allow myself to indulge in the usual manipulating game of role creation. Fortunately for me, my self-knowledge has transcended that and I have come to understand that life is best to be lived and not to be conceptualized. I am happy because I am daily growing and am honestly not knowing where the limit lies. To be certain, every day there can be a revelation or a new discovery.'

Another thought:

'I treasure the memory of the past misfortunes. It has added more to my bank of fortitude.'

And:

'My first love is martial art. By martial art, I mean an unrestricted athletic expression of an individual soul. Martial art also means daily hermit-like physical training to upgrade or maintain one's quality. To live is to express one's self freely in creation. Creation, I must say, is not a fixed something or a solidification. So I hope my fellow martial artists will open up and be transparently real and I wish them well in their own process of finding their cause.'

When I read Bruce's words about his hermit-like physical training in order to achieve merit and quality, I think of the many nights I awoke in the small hours and found my husband, his restless mind and energies still burning so fiercely that he could not sleep, busy at his stretching exercises, striving to drive his body and muscles towards new goals that only he could perceive; goals that he realized could never come any nearer— for as he reached one new level of perfection or achievement, another still lay ahead of him. . . .

'This article expresses my personal true beliefs, a sort of personal view of the motion picture industry and the ideas of an actor as well as a human being,' he wrote. 'Above all, I have to take responsibility to myself and do whatever is right. The script has to be right, the director has to be right, my time must be devoted to preparation of the role . . . after that comes money. To the business people in films—and I have to say that cinema is a marriage of art and business—the actor is not a human being but a product, a commodity. However as a human being. I have the right to be the best god damn product that ever walked, and work so hard that the business people have to listen to you. You have that personal obligation to yourself to make yourself the best product available according to your own terms. Not the biggest or the most successful, but the best quality—with that achieved comes everything else.

'An actor is, first of all, like you and me, a human being who is equipped with the capability to express himself psychologically and physically with realism and appropriateness, hopefully in good taste, which simply means the revelation of the sum total of all that he is—his tastes, his education, his individual uniqueness, his soul-searching experiences, his idiosyncrasies, etc. Just as no two human beings are alike, the same holds true for an actor.

'An actor is a dedicated being who works damn hard so that his level of understanding makes him a qualified artist in self-expression—physically, psychologically and spiritually. I regard acting as an art much like my practice in martial art because it is an expression of the self.

'As an actor I am frustrated between business and art with the hope that through harmonious reconciliation of these I can then come out expressing myself and truthfully communicating.

'Dedication, absolute dedication, is what keeps one ahead—a sort of indomitable obsessive dedication and the realization that there is no end or limit to this because life is simply an ever-growing process, an ever-renewing process.

159

'An actor, a good actor that is, is an artist with depth and subtlety. Indeed, what the audience sees on the screen is the sum total of what that particular human being's level of understanding is. If he is ready, well-prepared, radiating of tremendous force of energy, an honest confidence of expression, working hard to grow and expand oneself in one's own process; well, this person is a professional, an "efficient deliverer" in my book.'

An 'efficient deliverer'—that, too, was important to Bruce. Adrian Marshall remembers that once when they were sparring, Bruce 'tied me up like a pretzel so that I couldn't move. I stood there, totally frustrated—whatever I tried, Bruce could counter it with ease. "Try something else", commanded Bruce. "What?" I shouted angrily, "What *can* I do?" "You could always bite", laughed Bruce. But he meant it. In one of his films, the villain ties *him* up—in a wrestling hold. So what does he do—he bites! That was Bruce.' Efficiency was whatever scored. And the scorer was the 'efficient deliverer'. And if anybody ever delivered, he did.

TEN

James Coburn says that, toward the end of his life, Bruce seemed to be 'carrying a great weight . . . something had set in. He was being hit on all sides by everybody . . . and he had to have his guard up all the time.'

Lo Wei told Hong Kong newspapers that Bruce had tried to wound him with a knife. 'If I had wanted to kill Lo Wei,' scoffed Small Dragon, 'I would not have used a knife; two fingers would have been enough.'

Critics hit out at his use of nunchuks in *Fists of Fury*: 'I had to use some sort of weapons,' Bruce pointed out. 'After all, that guy was coming for me with a sword, and no man can use bare fists against swords' —he used to emphasize that, in real life, he was as vulnerable as anyone to any thug who crept up behind him from a dark alleyway.

His second film had made Bruce probably the hottest property in the entire world of show business. In the Philippines, for instance, the film ran for more than six months and the Government there finally had to limit the amount of foreign imports to protect their own domestic producers. In Singapore, as in Hong Kong itself, the scalpers made a fortune out of the film, charging £18 for a ticket worth just under £1. On opening night, so many fans rushed the cinema that an immense traffic snarl was set up with the result that the showing had to be suspended for a week while the police worked out new traffic arrangements. Producers all over the Orient began offering Bruce money; some making their offers through the medium of newspaper headlines—a cheap way for many, no doubt, to cash in on his publicity. 'I had a heck of a problem,' admitted Bruce to *Fighting Stars,* 'I had people stop by my door and just pass me a check for $200,000. When I asked them what it was for they replied, "Don't worry, it's just a gift to you." I mean, I didn't even know these people, they were strangers to me.' He said that he had become so confused that he became totally suspicious of everyone; feeling he could trust nobody any longer. 'It was very bewildering. I didn't know whom to trust and I even grew suspicious of my old pals. I was in a period when I didn't know who was trying to take advantage of me.

'When people pass out big money—just like that, you don't know what to think. I destroyed all those checks but it was difficult to do, because I didn't know what they were for.' He emphasized, 'Sure, money is important in providing for my family, but it isn't everything.'

There were other pressures—pressures of a more sordid nature. Any time he had his picture taken with an actress, wherever it might be, some scandal sheet would make up a story to the effect that he was having an affair with the girl.

After his death, there was no holding some of the scandal sheets—they had a field day. They simply concocted stories—mentioning this woman and that. This was the first time I had ever given a thought to the idea, 'is my husband fooling around?' And all I can honestly say is that if he were, I knew nothing about it. All I know is that he made me very happy; he was a good husband and a good father.

Certainly, I have to admit that the temptation must have been there for him. He was extremely attractive to look at; and he was blessed with enormous sex appeal. He traveled a lot—he was away from home for long periods on location and so on. But none of it matters to me—and if he were alive today, my attitude would be exactly as it is now. Women, I know pursued him. I am not talking now of the usual silly letters all male superstars tend to receive. He dismissed that sort of letters or phone calls pretty peremptorily. If he were traveling somewhere and he was pursued by a female, he generally mentioned it to me—'My goodness, this woman, she wouldn't leave me alone'; it was as straightforward and natural as that.

I could understand it all, of course. Bruce had been always the type of man who attracts women—the hero type; he was part of the James Bond/Sean Connery syndrome, if you like. I felt very fortunate that I happened to be married to him. He was a very outgoing personality, of course, and I got used to seeing women at public functions coming up and putting their arms around him or giving him a kiss or a hug; it's all part of show business, you know; what the British, I think, call a kind of a professional mateyness. I never felt any pangs of jealousy on such occasions, possibly because I had this attitude—'Go ahead—but I get to take him home.'

I don't suppose I ever let myself think too much about it really; we were too busy living our lives, worrying and thinking about Bruce's career and that kind of thing.

162

Once or twice during our nine-year marriage, we did discuss this whole question of the attitude of men and women to fidelity. Bruce did say that if ever he had an affair with another woman, it would be something that happened spontaneously; that he would never plan it or decide to have a mistress or anything of that nature. And if it happened, he added, it would never be more than a one-time thing; an accident caused by the circumstances of the moment. He added, 'If that ever happens, and if you ever find out about it I want you to know that it has absolutely no importance at all.' And he was very sweet and considerate when he said that and told me how important I was to him; how important his children were to him. He made me feel I was his special treasure. Infidelity, he suggested, had no real bearing on a marriage; the fleeting attraction for another female had no significance in regard to a matter so fundamental as a marriage. I remember saying, 'Oh, yeah?'

'Men are like that,' he said.

'Hmm?'

I have no idea—nor do I care—whether Bruce had been unfaithful when we had this conversation. It was so obvious to me that he really cared about me and about the children that a matter of that nature simply never worried me. I remember once where in the case of a couple we knew, the man had gone off to live with his mistress and the wife had just hung around forlornly for years displaying her misery and courting everyone's sympathy. I told him, 'If that ever happened between us, I'd be gone—like a flash.'

He looked a little surprised for my voice was firm and emphatic.

'*Would* you?' he asked, a little nonplussed.

'You're darned right, I would,' I said. And he knew I meant it.

I can do nothing to stamp out gossip, of course; I can only protest that if Bruce ever had affairs, then I was never hurt. What concerned me—and what I consider far more to the point than whether he ever allowed an ordinary human instinct to overwhelm him—was that his family was of supreme importance to him. He talked about that a lot, I may say; and when he talked, it was with a conviction and an honesty of expression that bore the stamp of total truth. He talked about this deep thing close to his heart when we were having pretty hard times; when there was pressure on him; when we were down—when he had hurt his back and his whole future looked black. When we discussed how important it was to him that he had security, I would often say to him that perhaps it would have been a lot easier for him to achieve his goals if he had not had the responsibility of me and the children. I remember him saying, 'No matter what, no matter how bad times are or how bad they become, I want you to know that the most important

Bruce Lee, superstar, at the height of his fame, in action in the world-wide smash hit, "Enter The Dragon." (Warner Bros.)

thing in my life is to have you and the children around me.' And I knew he meant it. In a way our marriage was bound to work, for, temperamentally, we were opposites. He was Bruce; an extraordinary human being, full of vitality and a tremendous extrovert, with high passions and an air of suppressed excitement and electrical discharges about his person; I, on the other hand, was quiet, calm—on hand when I was needed, full, I believe, of the security and reassurance that a highly-charged man like Bruce always needed. We were complementary to each other, in every sense. After all, he had to marry somebody with a different temperament. Now if he and I had been of similar natures?— well, one of us would have killed the other, such would

have been the turbulence, I feel. And the victim? Scarcely Bruce, I think.

I have quoted some of the poems Bruce wrote—some of them were obviously his own original efforts, others were clearly translations from the Chinese. They reveal, I believe, an innately sensitive and artistic nature. For he was never a sentimental or mushy man; he hated sentimentality. Emotional, yes; emotion and high intelligence; a finely-tuned scholar's brain.

In those last two years of his life, he often came home from the studios very boisterous, wrought-up, highly-charged about whatever the problem happened to be at that moment. He would go on about it; about how he felt; what he thought should be done—I realized he was in a very emotional state. He often felt compelled to get on the phone to discuss it with someone; he was unable to leave the problem alone. So I would try to help to work out whatever was wrong—perhaps by getting in touch with the right person. Sometimes he seemed baffled and frustrated because it had become physically impossible to get something done and it was around this stage that he began to sleep badly. When he was at the studios and something was going wrong, he used to telephone and ask me to go over; I don't think I ever did much to alleviate the situation but, just by being around, I think I had a calming effect. On the whole I believe we each did what was required of us in relation to the other. We played our separate roles as best we could and perhaps surprised each other by surpassing expectations we had never felt justified in entertaining; for as Bruce often quoted, 'I'm not in this world to live up to your expectations and you're not in this world to live up to mine.' Although I always had total confidence in him, even I, in the end, found that he had more than lived up to my most secret hopes.

He was a spontaneous person. He did not believe in having his life and actions circumscribed by conventions, particularly those foisted on populations by shrewd commercial interests. For instance, he ignored such occasions as St. Valentine's Day and Mother's Day, events nurtured by businessmen who see such days as opportunities to sell gifts, flowers, cards and so on. He sometimes forgot my birthday—though he was generally very good about our wedding anniversary. But he made up for it all by the sheer spontaneity of his behavior. When he arrived home, he frequently brought flowers, or candies—or, perhaps, even an expensive dress. He would have bought whatever it was on the spur of the moment—but it was the very element of surprise that made it all so delightful.

Once Bruce had finished *Big Boss* and *Fists of Fury,* he was on his own; under contract to no one. The success of *Boss* and *Fury* made Bruce aware that he must make a picture that would merit a greater public response and at the same time command more respect in the martial arts world. He'd had a long and hard struggle to get where he had arrived at but he knew that it was hard to stay at the top; that even more strenuous efforts would be necessary. He had seriously considered another Golden Harvest script, *The Yellow Faced Tiger,* but decided to let it go. It was a time of decision. He had to decide about his personal statement in regard to kung fu films. He was never satisfied to ride along on success; each film, he believed, would have been better than its predecessor. And he felt the only way he could achieve this was if he had more control over all the elements. He decided to form his own production company, Concord, and work in partnership with Raymond Chow.

He had been always dissatisfied with the way films were made in Hong Kong where the directors more or less make up the stories as they go along, based on a rough sketch or outline, in turn often based (but never acknowledged) on a *melange* of other old films or the innumerable pulp-type fantasy stories which pass for 'writing' in parts of Asia. Bruce insisted that there should be a proper script along Hollywood lines if he

167

were to do *Tiger*; when Lo Wei refused to agree, Bruce bowed out. It was a risk—but 'greatness requires the taking of risks; that's why so few ever achieve it'.

He bought several books about film-making and brushed up on his behind-the-scenes techniques. He felt there wasn't any 'soul' in Mandarin movies; that they were just running them off the assembly line and was determined to put his own stamp on all his films. So he decided, on pure guts alone, to write, direct, produce and star—to really do the whole thing himself. Which was really an extraordinarily gutsy thing to do. And once he had made his decision. I don't think he worried about the outcome. He assumed full responsibility and plunged into work like a man possessed.

One reason behind his decision was a burning desire to give each character he played in each film a distinctively different personality. He realized that people wanted to see him as a fighter, but his characters had to have greater depth, to have individual personality. No other actor in Hong Kong had ever taken such a step. He was as great a non-conformist with regard to Hong Kong films as he was with his ideas on the martial arts. He was an innovator; a creator—a man who shaped rather than was shaped by events.

Bruce finally hit on the main idea of the script for *The Way of the Dragon* (released elsewhere as *Return of the Dragon*) and then the development took place over many weeks of discussion. He made trips to location sites and had hours of discussion with the assistant director at our house. I sat in on most of this but as the conversations were generally conducted in Chinese, I cannot say I made much of a contribution. Later, we would talk over the ideas in English when we were alone—and they would help spark off new ideas for him.

From the beginning, he was aware that movie-making is a mixture of art and commercialism. Bringing the champion U.S. karate men. Chuck Norris and Bob Wall to Hong Kong and Italy was an aesthetic decision as well as a commercial one. The truly commercial aspect

168

was that the audience to which he was trying to appeal was Chinese—and the Chinese like to see their Chinese heroes conquering people of a different race. If that sounds like racial prejudice, it is understandable in view of their history. But just as important to Bruce was the fact that he would be tackling professional *karateka* rather than actors or dancers, which he believed would give his film added tension and authenticity.

To many who saw the film, perhaps the oddest thing of all was that a film about Chinese kung fu should be set in Rome; that the climax should take place in that ancient home of the gladiatorial arts, the Colosseum. But when Raymond Chow, Bruce's partner in the film, mentioned that he had a contact there who could arrange for equipment, locations and production details, Bruce at once spotted the piquant possibilities inherent in such a marvelous setting.

There were problems of logistics, time, permits and innumerable other difficulties to be overcome in Rome which, in the event, added to the film's veracity. They shot on the streets, at the airport, around Rome during traffic hours and even during bad weather. They shot between forty-five and sixty setups in Rome airport alone in one day. Bruce constantly demanded perfection of himself and everyone around him. No doubt some thought he was difficult to work with but he knew what he wanted—and how to get it. He could be very blunt and outspoken when he wanted to be—and he was all of that on his next picture, *Enter the Dragon*— but here he was patience itself with both actors and crew. For all his quick flare-ups, he kept his temper throughout. The schedule was unbelievably stiff—a fourteen-hour day, seven days a week. Within two weeks, the Rome scenes were in the can and the unit moved back to Hong Kong to shoot the rest of the film.

Staging the fight scenes was Bruce's specialty. They had to be super perfect. Each fight was planned on paper, each movement, each angle. For instance, the last big duel with Chuck Norris takes up twenty pages of written instructions. It was as carefully choreographed as a dance number. Bruce had worked it all out in our study at home—often with me playing Chuck Norris. He would get a sudden inspiration and yell, 'Come on, let's try this.' Then we'd try all the movements and he would write them all down—to help, he had one wall of the room covered in mirrors. We even worked out the best angles from which to shoot the sequences. He was always involved in thinking about new techniques because each fight had to be different from all his other fights—either in this or his other films.

He found fight scenarios really fascinating. In the three films he did up to and including *The Way of the Dragon*, there must have been about thirty fights. Each had to be different and had to fit into the character's personality. Then, with everything planned, the fights had to be tried out with his opponents—and such things as his adversary's strength, height and so on allowed for. He also used fresh weapons in this fight—a staff in one fight, two nunchuks in another. He also made and used darts. He intended to go on drawing on his superb knowledge of ancient and modern weapons, both Oriental and Western.

The fight scenes with some of the Caucasian players who were not real actors also took some working out. When they were hit, they had to have their reactions carefully choreographed. For, after all, nobody *really* gets hit. The blow only seems to be getting home, and this takes meticulous timing and much rehearsal. His martial arts performances for the screen, his choreography and his direction of other actors or martial artists was a skilled art, but it was not the kind of martial art he used in a defense situation.

When the film was finally released, it ran into a new situation in Hong Kong: censorship. A new anti-violence campaign had been opened (and, indeed, was copied by Singapore which heavily censored all violent Mandarin-language films, including *The Way of he Dragon*), but fortunately the censors insisted on cutting only one small scene (which was restored for overseas distribution) where Bruce lands five consecutive kicks to Chuck's head. It was a beautiful movement, an important part of the way the viewer is led into the psychology of the fight and it is a pity it had to go.

There was one other outstanding innovation in this film. Most Chinese films use canned music for their scores. But this one had its own special score with Bruce personally sitting in on one recording session and playing a percussion instrument. He had a supervising hand in everything—the dubbing, the set plans, the set building, choosing costumes and finally, editing the film. He must have seen the film several hundred times, either in bits or pieces or in its more or less finished version.

His original idea in making the film had been to show another side of himself to Hong Kong audiences —for when he first thought of the film, he had intended it for distribution in Southeast Asia only. He had no intention of aiming at the world market—so he constructed and produced a story that would appeal to Chinese people primarily. He also planned a very appealing character, that of a naïve country boy trying to adjust to situations in a crowded foreign capital; a character through whom he was able to show a very humorous side of himself; a side which had never appeared before in any of his films. I think he drew a great deal from his own experiences in drawing this character—recollecting those first days when he had returned to San Francisco, his birthplace, from Hong Kong. There is a lot of the real Bruce Lee personality and character in that film.

He made a wager that this film would outgross his first two films, at least in Hong Kong. He forecast that it would take more than five million HK dollars. Nobody could believe it—almost three times as much as *Sound of Music*. The press, when they heard of his wager, began to tease him unmercifully. Bruce threw himself into the fun of it and was almost schoolboyish in his glee when *The Way of the Dragon* finally topped the five million mark. Inevitably, it broke every record ever established on the Mandarin circuit.

At home, he had a videotape recorder attached to his TV set so that he could tape Western boxing and wrestling shows. He also bought up films of boxers such as Muhammad Ali in action. He used to run these through his editing machines, studying combat techniques, constantly thinking ahead to the fight scenes he would need for his next film . . . and the one after that . . . and after that . . . For Bruce, the hours of the day were meant for work; for achieving things. . . .

He told the *China Mail* that he enjoyed the simple, quiet life; which, by and large, was true. 'I don't feel like social gatherings,' he declared. 'Nor am I interested in publicizing myself. But such things are unavoidable in a star's life, particularly in a small place like Hong Kong.' What made it worse, he thought, was that there were too many people trying to be nice to him but he doubted that they were doing it out of friendship. He was sorry that the film bosses misunderstood him. 'They think I am only interested in money. That's why they all try to lure me onto their sets by promising me huge sums and nothing else. But at heart I only want a fair share of the profit. What I long for is to make a really good movie.' On the whole, we were both satisfied that he had achieved this with *The Way of the Dragon*. Some Westerners criticized the film as being naïve in plot and handling and with low production values. But Bruce realized that his audiences throughout Southeast Asia could not be reeducated overnight; that they could not be hurried. He knew instinctively the kind of film that appealed to them and that a big great glossy Hollywood-type movie would never have the same appeal. Events, as it transpired, were to prove him right.

ELEVEN

Perhaps the one thing that comes bouncing off the screen most in all of Bruce's films is his sheer animal magnetism. He had this tremendous energy, some inner force that seemed to grow stronger and more compelling the more he used it. Success, rather than dampening this force, seemed to give it a further kick. He told Adrian Marshall, 'I can feel it sort of bubbling and roaring up inside me.'

Outwardly while finishing off the dubbing and editing of *The Way of the Dragon* in Hong Kong, Bruce, unshaven and with a little mustache he often grew to disguise himself on the streets, was as sunny and bright as only he could be when the pressures were off. Interviewed by a Singapore journalist on the set, we get intimate glimpses of him as he would be glad, probably, to be remembered. As they walk through the studio, she writes, 'it soon becomes obvious that this idol of thousands in Asia is an extremely friendly person. Each of the studio hands we pass by is greeted with a "good morning" or "how are you today?" ' One man thus accosted turned out to be someone else. 'Sorry,' Bruce sings out, 'case of mistaken identity, but good morning all the same.' He makes jokes; massages the neck of a young lady assistant who has a crick in it; admits that he writes his scripts in Chinese first and has somebody else 'polish it up a bit' later as his Chinese is getting a little rusty. He whistles his favorite tune and announces, 'I'd like to teach the world to sing' and then adds, 'But if there's one thing I'm certain of, it is the fact that I can't sing. I tell people I have a rich voice—because it is well off!' He plays tricks with dollar notes: he gives fighting lessons to a few friends, counseling them, 'You must be fierce, but have patience at the same time. Most important of all, you must have complete determination. The worst opponent you can come across is one whose aim has become an obsession. For instance, if a man has decided that he is going to bite off your nose no matter what happens to him in the process, the chances are he will succeed in doing it. He may be severely beaten up but that will not stop him carrying out his original objective. That is the real fighter.' He hurls anathema at gossips—'people in Hong Kong gossip too much'. A photographer arrives to take pictures and asks if Bruce will work for the Shaw Brothers—he tells the man, 'If I have a good script I will consider it. I want to be neutral and act for whichever company can provide me with good scripts. I don't want to be involved in any conflicts or competition here.' Within minutes, there are six photographers on the scene, all asking the same question. Irritated, Bruce snaps, 'Tell them I've signed for twenty films with the Shaws.'

Later, he revealed something of the dilemma in which he found himself. 'I can do what I like usually in a film. But it also has set limitations. People expect me to fight. They expect action. So in a way I am imprisoned by my own success.' He talked openly and frankly in a way that may not have endeared him to everyone. He talked about the 'cultural gap' between East and West; criticized production standards in Hong Kong; claimed that too many in the industry 'were not professional enough'. He thought some of the Hong Kong 'stars' missed their 'considerable power'. He talked about his own pitfalls—the great sums to make TV commercials; the constant offers to make films—'it would not be fair to anyone if I start shooting a dozen films a year'. He declared vehemently, 'What I detest most is dishonest people who talk more than they are capable of doing. I also find people obnoxious who use false humility as a means to cover their inadequacy.' He admitted that his long sojourn in America meant that he 'opened to people naturally' but found 'There is the other group of people who try to utilize me for their own ends. There was this producer who insisted that I go along to see the rushes of his new film. To oblige him I did. The next thing I knew advertisements for the film proclaimed in bold print that Bruce Lee had spoken highly of the production.'

It would be entirely wrong to suggest that Bruce, in some strange and fateful way, had not found happiness. He was as happy, in most respects, as it is possible for any human to be. Yet he was never misled by the nature of what had happened to him. His sudden fame and fortune he described as 'illusive creations and impostors' and he revealed his sincere thoughts in a letter he wrote privately to his old friend Mito Uyehara, publisher of *Black Belt*, dealing with his new pressures and responsibilities:

'After reading your article on me, I have mixed feelings. To many, the word "success" seems to be a paradise but now that I'm in the midst of it, it is nothing but circumstances that seem to complicate my innate feelings towards simplicity and privacy. Yet, like it or not, circumstances are thrust upon me and, being a fighter at heart, I sort of fight it in the beginning but soon realize what I need is not inner resistance and needless conflict in the form of dissipation; rather, by joining forces to re-adjust and make the best of it.

'I can't go wrong because what I've always liked in myself is this "stickability" towards quality and the sincere desire to do it right. In a way, I am glad that this prosperous happening is occurring to me when I am maturing to a state of readiness and definitely will not blow it because of "self-glorification" or being "blinded by illusions," I am prepared.

'Well, my dear friend—lately friend has come to be a scarce word, a sickening game of watchfulness towards offered friendship—I miss you and our once simple lunches together and our many joyful communications.

'Take care and have fun—hope you are still jogging, which is the only form of relaxation to me nowadays.'

175

I think that letter alone is sufficient to dispose of at least two canards which have been spread abroad about Bruce; that for all his success, he had few friends; and again, that he tended to forget them. I suppose no man has more than half-a-dozen *real* friends throughout his life and Bruce was more fortunate than most. And he remembered them. Taky Kimura went through a severe domestic crisis shortly before Bruce died. At first he had been reluctant to let Bruce know about it—Bruce, after all, was now a great film star and on the way to becoming a millionaire and 'I didn't want to be known as a hanger-on.' To his astonishment, Bruce telephoned him from Hong Kong and chided him: 'Look, I'm the same guy I've always been. If there is ever anything you need just ask me.' And he wrote Taky a long letter which the latter says 'helped me go through an emotional state successfully'.

It had been Bruce's intention after he had finished *The Way of the Dragon* to take a short rest and then start work on a film called *The Game of Death*. No script had been yet worked out but he had a vague idea which would involve gathering some of the world's greatest martial artists and athletes together. Then he heard that his old friend, Kareem Abdul Jabbar, the American basketball star, was paying a visit to Hong Kong. Bruce wrote to him and suggested that they should do a scene together. He had decided that almost nothing could be more intriguing then to see him battling against a man almost *two* feet taller. Kareem agreed enthusiastically and for about a week they planned and then shot some of the most fantastic and most beautiful fight scenes ever filmed.

As I write this, *The Game of Death* remains an uncompleted film. When Bruce shot those fight scenes, he had nothing but the vaguest semi-structure in mind. Gradually over the months ahead, this semi-structure was improved on. The basis of the story concerns a treasure kept on the top floor of a pagoda in Korea. It was a pagoda where martial artists were trained and each floor was devoted to training a different style of

176

martial art. In the part of the film that was eventually completed, Bruce had to go into the pagoda with two followers and to fight his way up through the floors, tackling a different martial artist and a different style on each floor. Danny Inosanto, who uses the nunchuka as well as anyone now alive, defended one floor. A Korean 7th degree Hapkido Chi Hon Joi defended another floor and so on. Right at the top was Kareem Abdul Jabbar, the final protector of the treasure. The fight between them, as I have said, is quite extraordinary. It has often been argued that if Bruce were locked in a room with Muhammad Ali and both were allowed to fight in their usual styles, then Bruce was bound to have been the winner. Kareem, I know, would never pretend that he is a boxer—yet the problems posed to Bruce by an opponent's over-towering height and the way he combats them make marvelous film.

As the movie now stands, only the fight sequences have been shot. A satisfactory story line still remains to be constructed and the problem of shooting a large part of the film without Bruce's actual presence must somehow be overcome. I can only say that there will be no substitute for Bruce.

The fight scenes for *The Game of Death* took their toll even of Bruce's seemingly inexhaustible reservoir of energies, coming as they did on top of his extremely hard work with *The Way of the Dragon*. Nonetheless, he settled down happily to work out the script details. At the same time, the offers flooded in. Run Run Shaw offered an open contract (later a figure of 2.5 million HK dollars was agreed). Carlo Ponti and other Italian producers cabled offers. A Hungarian producer in Hong Kong got into the act, as well as producers from all over the Orient. There were offers from several Hollywood studios, including MGM, who wanted Bruce to co-star with Elvis Presley, but Bruce was determined to wait for his own special vehicle.

'It's like I'm in jail,' Bruce said, 'I'm like a monkey in the zoo. People looking at me and things like that, and basically I like simple life and I like to joke a lot and all those things. But I cannot speak as freely as before, because misinterpretation comes in and all kinds of things, you know.

'It hasn't changed me basically, because I know that in my process of being born and going to die something happened which is breaking some records. To me, it doesn't mean anything. It's just something that happens. It's not that I'm proud or better than I ever was, I'm just the same damn old shit.'

Whatever he thought he was, he was something that Hollywood could no longer ignore. It had not taken long for word to spread that Bruce's films had grossed more than *The Godfather* or *Sound of Music* in many of the most important areas of the world. Bruce dealt with the offers from an office at the Golden Harvest studios in Hammer Hill Road, Kowloon, where he kept a seemingly out-of-place pair of old broken spectacles. As he explained to a reporter, 'to remind me of the days when I was so broke I couldn't even afford a pair of new glasses' (Bruce wore glasses when studying).

Bruce *wanted* Hollywood to approach him. With the *rapprochement* between China and the United States a new factor in world politics, he realized that his chances of breaking into the international market, of becoming the first Chinese world superstar in history, were no longer an impossible dream. The bamboo and dollar curtains had been pierced and America, still the greatest world cinema power was, he thought, ripe to accept an Oriental hero. The catalyst was Fred Weintraub, formerly vice president in charge of production at Warner Brothers. Weintraub had been responsible for such successes as *Woodstock,* George C. Scott's *Rage* and Jane Fonda's *Klute.* For four years, Fred Weintraub had dreamed of putting a good martial arts story on film. He had started off by trying to interest the company in a film three and a half years earlier but the studio had given him a flat no. Undeterred, he had commissioned a script entitled Kung Fu—which eventually became the basis of the successful TV show. Linking up with Paul

Heller, whose screen credits included Elizabeth Taylor's *Secret Ceremony*, Fred formed Sequoia Pictures and supervised the writing of a script by screenwriter Michael Allin called 'Blood and Steel,' which later became *Enter the Dragon*. 'There's an incomparable beauty that's like a deadly kind of ballet to the martial arts. Regardless of the hostility in them, one can't deny the thrill of watching a great fighter go through his paces,' explained Fred. Warner Brothers agreed to finance the production with Concord and the budget was 500,000 U.S. dollars (the film eventually cost over 800,000 U.S. dollars). This was relatively modest by Hollywood standards, but was a huge budget by Mandarin standards and was a staggering triumph for Bruce. There was no question, either, about who would star.

By February 1973, Fred, Heller, director Robert Clouse, John Saxon, Jim Kelly, the 1971 International Middleweight Karate Champion, the beautiful actress Ahna Capri, and Bob Wall (who was to play the villainous Oharra) had joined Bruce in Hong Kong for thirteen grueling weeks' shooting. Hong Kong took some of the cast by surprise. Jim Kelly was surprised at the high crime rate and the toughness of the teen-age gangs. He told *Fighting Stars*: 'I thought the teen-age gangs in the U.S. were tough but they're real tame compared to those in Hong Kong. The gang, I think they are called "Triads", is vicious.' He was even more impressed by the fact that although the Chinese in Hong Kong often had very little money, he found long lines for martial arts films. 'No matter what people say, credit for this wave of interest in the martial arts movie has to go to Bruce Lee. Bruce is heavy. He's responsible for the present rage for martial arts movies. I've told him personally that I think highly of him for what he is. He's not only good in technique, but he's got a good analytical mind. He anaylzes everything he does, and this amazes me. Naturally, I have to respect him for being the most successful person that came up through the ranks in the martial arts field.' On a more personal level Bruce impressed him because 'he treats everyone the

179

same, even the kids. Kids in Hong Kong idolize him and I think this is good for them.'

Bob Wall explained why he liked the story. 'It was honest and totally believable. More important, it was not detrimental to the martial arts. It involved a tournament held on an island fortress. Han, a ruthless heroin dealer, invites American karate experts William (Jim Kelly) and Roper (John Saxon) to participate in the tournament. Lee (Bruce), a Shaolin Temple martial arts student, refuses to enter the tournament at first, then changes his mind when he discovers that several of Han's men, led by Oharra—that's me—had attacked his sister and had caused her to commit suicide during the last tournament.

'The island, as it turns out, is not only the headquarters for a giant heroin cartel, it's also a place where girls are kept for "experiments" and sale. Although Lee has stifled his desire to revenge his sister, Oharra is no match for Lee's lightning-fast feet. Infuriated, Oharra grabs two bottles, breaks them and lunges at Lee. Lee finally has no choice but to kill Oharra.

'It's not just another of those eye-for-an-eye stories. Actually Lee is portrayed as a non-violent man. Up to the time he kills Oharra he uses only as much power as necessary for the moment. The theme definitely is in keeping with the principles of martial arts.' Bob was enthusiastic about Bruce's behind-the-scene role: 'He's not only a great martial artist, he's a good actor as well as a good technician. He believes in spontaneity. After instructing us in what to do in the fight scenes, we shot them over and over until he felt it looked very exciting. As a martial artist, it's not fun to be on the receiving end of kicks and punches without being able to retaliate. But working with Bruce taught me to take the punches and kicks without hurting myself and yet make them look authentic. Of course, the fact that Bruce has perfect control of his blows makes it even more reassuring.' Wall describes one sequence with Bruce as follows: 'Bruce wanted me to jump, spin and back-kick at his head. As anyone in the martial arts knows, that's not easy. To make it even harder Bruce wanted me to drop low and go over him as he drop kicks in my groin. It was a very difficult shot, but we did it over and over until it finally came out perfectly.

'But as if that wasn't enough, Bruce had me lunge at him with two broken bottles.'

It is not all that easy to detail or chronicle all the pressures that had begun bearing down on Bruce while he was making *Enter the Dragon* and in the opinion of most of us who were nearest to him, these led to intolerable physical and mental strain. It was as though he were a machine which had been revved up to its ultimate capacities. There were the sheer pressures of living in cramped Hong Kong with its constant physical challenges and dangerous violence; there was the scandal press bearing in on his privacy, seeking to create sensations of a most sordid kind; there were the producers and entrepreneurs of every type seeking to exploit him and his name; there was the sheer physical and mental strain of making his spectacular films; there were the creative drains on his energies and emotions—how to keep the balance between the demands of international stardom and the need to retain his Mandarin audiences: there was the future—what paths should he take? There was the strain of life in Hong Kong with its teeming millions, its terrible noise and the humidity which sapped even the fittest.

There were three violent physically or psychologically damaging incidents during the making of the film. None of them, taken alone, was more than trivial, but taken in the aggregate, they scarcely helped Bruce. The first was when he severely damaged his hands during a fight with Bob Wall. Bob has explained, 'I grabbed a bottle in each hand, smashed off the bottoms and got set. I looked down at the jagged ends; they were lethal weapons all right. I thought, "My God, they're using real glass!" It flew everywhere. I looked across at Bruce. He hadn't even flinched. He just quietly said, "Come ahead, come in at me". When I took a step I could hear the sugary crunch of the glass grinding underfoot. Then the fight that Bruce had so carefully choreographed began. It went off perfectly. He finally finished me off, and I fell, landing right there among all those pieces of broken glass. The director yelled "Cut!" and then we had to do the whole scene over again to shoot it all from another angle.'

All that glass you see shattering at the touch of a finger in Hollywood Westerns is, of course, not real glass. It is imitation glass made of sugar which would not harm a baby's bottom. In Hong Kong, however, such sophisticated (and expensive) devices are unknown. In choreographing his fight with Bob Wall, Bruce had worked out the moves with meticulous care. Unfortunately, during one of the takes of this fight scene, Bruce struck too quickly and Bob had not sufficient time to let go of the bottles. Bruce's flashing fists crashed into the jagged broken glass and blood spurted from the terrible gashes.

It was a week, in fact, before he could return to the set.

In another scene, Bruce has to get past a cobra. To everyone's horror, the cobra struck at Bruce and bit him. Fortunately, it had been devenomized; nevertheless, it was not a pleasant experience.

Adding to all the other pressures was the inevitable challenge from an extra who thought he could 'take' the master; to understand Bruce's position, it is only necessary to recall the fine Gregory Peck film called *The Gunfighter* where a veteran gunslinger, trying at last to find peace, discovers that his own reputation will never give him rest; every young punk in every town in which he finds himself, wants to gain 'glory' by being the man who gunned down the greatest gun in the West. Bruce had to avoid the streets of Hong Kong more than he would have liked because of this sort of thing. One extra had challenged him while working on *Fists of Fury* and Bruce had toyed with him long enough to convince him that he was wasting his time. On *Enter the Dragon*, there were hundreds of extras, most of them just young punks. One kept constantly challenging Bruce, yelling at him, 'I don't believe you can do everything you say you can.' Bruce, who had no need to prove his skill or his manhood, tried to ignore him and to turn the challenge into a jest. Finally, he told the fellow, 'I don't care what you think.'

The upshot was that the man began to brag that Bruce was afraid to fight him. Bruce put up with it until one day, when all the pressures had put him into a bad mood, he agreed to a match. Bruce struck quickly; the guy went down like a bowling pin with a bloody lip. But he got up, only to be knocked down again. Bruce's anger evaporated almost as quickly as it had erupted and he toyed with the chap until he gave up. It was not his intention to disable the guy, just to teach him a lesson. As usual, the local newspapers played the story up and according to their version, Bruce had knocked the guy almost unconscious. Some newspapers took a bitter delight in trying to egg Bruce on to fight his various challengers—often condemning him if he didn't.

In a sense, he could never win. If he accepted a challenge, he seemed a bully; if he refused it, he was made to appear a *poseur*. Whichever way it went, it was always a good 'story' for the newspapers.

The film was scheduled to be shot in four weeks— but took ten. Many of the circumstances could not have been foreseen—such as the accident to Bruce's hand. But I shall go into Bruce's part in everything a little later.

The story itself, as scripted by Michael Allin, was little more than a Chinese version of the Bond story *Dr. No.* Han, an ex-Shaolin priest, owns an island fortress and lives in strict secrecy, guarded by hundreds of fighters. He decides to hold a tournament and invites the world's best fighters. Lee (Bruce used his own name in the film) whose sister has been murdered by Oharra, Han's chief lieutenant, is asked to go and his teacher tells him to accept and restore the reputation of the Shaolin Temple. He goes, knowing who killed his sister. John Saxon and Jim Kelly, old friends, also go along. Once on the island, the comedy note quickly evaporates and suspense takes over. Bruce goes about his business, trying to gather information, helped by a beautiful young lady who is one of Han's servants. Jim Kelly is captured by Han's organization and accused of spying and killed in a bloody fight. Han later shows John Saxon around an underground factory, explaining to him that this is his drug operation and that he would like John to work for him as his representative in the U.S. The crunch comes when John turns around to find Jim Kelly strung up in shackles over a sinister looking pool into which he is dropped and vanishes. Meanwhile, Bruce is still prowling around and is assaulted by a mob of guards. With incredible skill he destroys them all. But in his attempt to escape, he is trapped by the cunning old Han.

At the tournament the following day, John is ordered by Han to kill Bruce but refuses and instead fights one of Han's henchmen and kills him. With that Bruce and John are attacked by the rest of Han's men, whom they manage to kill with the help of some released prisoners. Han makes his escape but not before attacking Bruce with a claw hand fixed into his empty wrist. Bruce follows him into what must be one of the most bizarre of torture chambers and they fight. The fight continues into a multi-mirrored room where eventually Bruce wins, leaving Han impaled on a spear.

The crew faced some daunting problems in making the film. Disorientation; jet fatigue; change of climate, food and culture—all had their effect. No one had really thought out the problems likely to be encountered, particularly the simple job of communicating with Chinese actors and extras. Everything, too, had to be constructed from scratch. Full scale props, boats, houses were all built by hundreds of Chinese craftsman and laborers. Seven praying mantises had to be flown in from Hawaii for a scene lasting only twenty seconds. The Americans were more than impressed by the Chinese ability to construct elaborate sets without power tools and other aids taken for granted in Hollywood. But the language problems added to delays, as did different social customs. An assistant prop man forgot to bring a prop one morning and he was so ashamed that he vanished and didn't come back for three days. He had lost face, which is a disgrace to a Chinese. Some days it took hours just to position the three hundred extras and explain what they had to do. Often, after finishing a day with explanations of the next day's shooting, half the extras failed to turn up. There was difficulty finding women to play 'extra' roles and so the director Robert Clouse hired some of Hong Kong's 'escort' girls for the parts. But they also proved unreliable.

Also, people fell sick or got injured. One actor was almost drowned when filming from a junk in the choppy seas.

In one or two of the sequences, Bruce's movements were so fast that the camera had to be speeded up to several notches higher than its normal speed (the faster the camera is cranked, the slower the motion on the screen). Clouse maintained that Bruce's performance surprised him: 'He's a good actor as well as a supreme martial artist.' Kurt Hirshler, who edited the film, declared, 'I got a genuine education working with footage of Bruce Lee. He's so lightning fast and yet everything he does is perfect.' Although he could slow down the film or stop it as he pleased to observe Bruce's movements, he added, 'There aren't even signals he gives—not a hint that he's going to throw a punch. He's also in possession of incredible energy. He'd often have to do ten or fifteen takes of one fight scene, and he'd rarely show any fatigue. I got tired just watching him on film as I edited it.'

Fred Weintraub felt that in many respects they were all extremely lucky to finish the film even inside ten weeks. 'It was completely different to Hollywood. The Chinese say yes to everything, but they don't mean yes. They have no sense of the way we make pictures in Hollywood—their pictures have no continuity and no one cares. Instead of editing, they do their cuts in the camera. They don't bother to cover each scene from a lot of angles.' He found it impossible to record sound

185

directly on the set because in all Mandarin movies, sound is dubbed in afterward. 'It was impossible to keep crew and cast quiet during shooting,' he says.

It seems time, therefore, to look a little deeper at what really took place behind the scenes. Fred Weintraub and I have recently had a long discussion about it and what follows is a distillation of our very long conversation.

TWELVE

Fred Weintraub had known Bruce for some time even before we went to live in Hong Kong. He recalls: 'I knew Bruce as a very quiet and considerate person—I remember on my birthday once, Bruce dashed all the way down to Chinatown to buy me a set of nunchuka. I found him interesting—indeed, everyone was fascinated by his martial arts skill. Linda was very different, though, quiet, but firm. Bruce was a really nice guy at that time.

'He was undoubtedly nervous about *Enter the Dragon* —apprehensive. A lot was riding on it—it was his first big international film. He was under tremendous pressure—he and the writer Michael Allin just didn't see eye to eye. In addition he was on his home ground and I think he wanted to avoid giving the impression of partiality towards Americans, of favoring them at the expense of his own ethnic group. So there was this dichotomy operating for him. And on the whole, he wanted the film to be more Chinese than American. Which was very understandable.

'On the set, however, he was truly professional— really outstanding. That was after we had finally got him on. It took us two to three weeks before he finally showed up. Meanwhile, I'm getting these hysterical cables from Warner Brothers—where's Bruce?

'Eventually he did show up. And the first thing that happened was that he walked off the set on the very first day. This was after he had had a fight with Raymond Chow. The film was supposed to be a joint Concord (Bruce's and Raymond's company)–Sequoia (Weintraub and Heller's company)–Warner Bros. production. This newspaper had it that it was a Golden Harvest production. So Bruce called Raymond Chow and then walked off.'

I can only say that Bruce was under enormous emotional pressure; was the film going to be good enough or not? He would go into his study and just disappear and think about it. He had to make sure everything was just right even before he started—for if it weren't, then he could always back out. He *would* have backed out, I think. But he was certainly distraught at times. At one moment, he would be feeling real high and ready to go. Ten minutes later, he would be in the depths of depression about it all. As Fred puts it, "I had to 'psych' him at times."

'I think he was kinda hibernating in those first few weeks; I think he was terribly frightened,' insists Fred. 'Here he had his big chance—and there's no question but that he would have been the biggest superstar if he had lived, for he had this thing that happens to great performers on screen—it's a kind of magnetism. It's the same with guys like Clint Eastwood—just a nice guy when you meet him at a party but something unique and special when he gets on the screen.

'About our differences—well, first, the script could never have been to his liking. He and the writer just didn't see eye to eye. So I just went ahead and shot sequences even though Bruce wasn't ready to start. I kept telling Warner Brothers he was going to show up every day—for Linda had told me that eventually he would. And she was right.

'I found him very different from the guy I'd known in Los Angeles. He was a major star now—and he be-

187

haved just like all major stars in this business. He was all right once he saw Bob Clouse directing—throughout the picture about the only two people he would talk to were Bob and Linda. I tried to keep the whole thing on a strictly producer-star footing.

'He was nervous the first day we actually started shooting. You could see him twitching—Bob Clouse said to me, "He's twitching." That first scene with him was a very simple one but it took twenty takes. Then he just quieted down and from there on he was fantastic. Once he saw the rushes—from then on, he was really professional.

'But there were real nervous worries before we got him to that point. Warner Brothers kept sending all these new scripts, hoping we'd get one that Bruce would like. There we were—twelve days into the picture and another script arrived from Hollywood. I rang them and said "I've had enough—I'm on my way home." Then Linda called and said, "It's going to be all right tomorrow." And it was.

'It was not easy for him—and I don't think anybody can be glib about it. You can't dismiss it as ego tripping or anything like that. Here he was, the greatest martial artist-actor of them all, lining up, as it were, for the Olympics. It was the big moment—all he had been striving for. I got the impression that somewhere or other along the line in the U.S. Bruce felt he had been shunted—that the guys like Coburn and McQueen considered him as a teacher, but never considered him as a major screen personality; and suddenly here he had his chance to outshine them all. Certainly, after *Enter the Dragon,* his price would have been at least five times as much as Jim Coburn could command. Even in the American market, he would have been bigger than McQueen—certainly *Enter the Dragon* did better business than McQueen's *The Getaway*—and this was what Bruce was dying to do. He wanted to prove he had been right. That he wasn't a crazy man.

'Once he got rolling—once he got his foot in the water, so to speak, he was dynamic and came up with several great ideas. But he got terribly upset when he hurt his hand on the bottles.

'Remember that never in history had a Chinese had his name above the title of an American film. Everything was riding on it. And somewhere in the middle of it all, there were these people talking about "foreign devils"— there was a lot of talk by the Chinese, a lot of anti-Americanism—here were the "foreign devils" horning in on a Chinese art. So when he got his hand hurt, he felt it was a sort of portent.'

In fact, Bruce was as upset about allowing himself to get hurt by the bottles as the pain and injury themselves; after all, as a consummate martial artist, he felt he should have been able to avoid the bottles whatever Bob Wall did. He had always been so accurate. He was in no sense paranoiac nor neurotic—and he knew too much about what was happening in his own head to permit himself to drift from his central theme. He was simply wound-up and highly strung about it all.

Bruce died before *Enter the Dragon* was ever released. The picture had gone way above budget, but, when Warner Brothers first saw it, they knew they had a winner and gave Fred authority to spend fifty thousand U.S. dollars for special music and sound effects.

Fred says: 'Bruce had no real idea, I think, of just how big the picture was going to be. Certainly, it surprised Warner Brothers. I think it's going to be a classic film—and I've advised against ever releasing it on TV. I think it will come back every three or four years for the rest of time, because Bruce is no longer here and if you want to see him, then you've got to see this film. There's a whole cult growing up around him—and I think it will grow bigger rather than die away. It won't date the way the Bond films have—because it didn't rely on scientific gadgetry which will date. Think of it—it broke all records in Japan, which is traditionally the worst market in the world for Chinese films. Most Chinese films are anti-Japanese and everybody felt the Japanese would reciprocate—but they didn't.

'I believe Bruce would have earned a million dollars

a film on his next picture—on his salary alone. He was pure dynamite. He was an "exploitation star" the way John Wayne, Clint Eastwood and Cary Grant in his own *milieu* were.

'He would have been very strong. He had a warmth. He was a very lonely guy—he kept himself aloof from people. I found in my own opinion that he was terribly lonely, and except for Linda he trusted nobody in this world. Linda was the only one he would talk to, or trust, or have confidence in; she was wife, mother, mistress, lover, everything . . . he would never talk to anyone else. If he didn't want to talk to somebody, he made Linda talk to them. If he were angry, he made Linda call them up and say "I'm angry". If he had a fight, he would have Linda call. He would never call up and apologize personally, you know. He'd have her call up—but not to apologize; but to say, "Well, it's all over now, it's okay." He knew when he had done wrong—it wasn't a question of right or wrong. Bruce always knew right and wrong—it was just that he didn't want to face up to it.'

This was true. Bruce would come home and say to me when he had cooled off a little, 'Well, maybe I was a little too hasty—why don't you call up?'

'Yes, why don't you do the dirty work and call up,' says Fred, laughing. 'I'd say he was lonely in a sense; he was a loner—but that's the quality that makes a star in a funny way. I mean all that intensity that was part of his personality, it came through on the screen. He could have done a great love story in my opinion. Because he had so much inside him, it was just a question of giving it out. Off screen, certainly, he'd take off his shirt and show you his muscles and all that—he'd show his punching and so on; but in Hong Kong at that time, towards the end, he never gave you as much in person as he was capable of giving. He always kept you a little at arm's length—you were always one step away from meeting Bruce Lee, the real Bruce Lee. The only time you saw the real man I think, was when you saw him playing with his kids. Everything would change then; everything would be different.

'Yes, Bruce had so much. I remember one night, Bruce and I were having dinner with Senator John Tunney, a very important man in America. His father, of course, was the great Gene Tunney who beat Jack Dempsey. Now, not many people of Bruce's generation knew that Gene Tunney had written a couple of books after he retired as undefeated heavyweight champion and Senator Tunney was flabbergasted. . . .'

By the end of April 1973, Bruce had more or less made up his mind that he would return to live in the United States where things were easier and there were more opportunities, returning perhaps twice a year or so to Hong Kong to make a film there because there he would have all the control and freedom that he needed. Fantastic offers were now flooding in on him and I can only describe it as a time of great indecision. He often said that the distractions of fame and success, of being in the public eye all the time, where creating a dissipation of energy. He treated the whole thing as an irritation, though, rather than as a really serious matter, because his own focus, his own knowledge of where he wanted to go and how he was going to get there, was always very, very strong.

Nonetheless, he was shrewd enough to know when and where to seek the right advice. Ted Ashley, Chairman of the Board of Warner Brothers, had been a friend of long standing, so immediately after *Enter the Dragon* had been completed (but before its actual release) he wrote a heartfelt letter to Ted:

'Ted,
'Nowadays, my offers for doing a film have reached a point which I guarantee you will both surprise as well as shock you. Viewing from the angle of efficient practical business sense, I hope we will be fair and square and have mutual trust and confidence—I have had a bad experience doing a picture with some per-

son or organization in Hong Kong. In other words, I was burned once, and didn't like it.

'Without Bruce Lee, I am sure that Warner Bros. will definitely and factually suffer no loss, and vice versa; therefore, and I sincerely mean it, that is from one human being to another, practical business or whatever it is, I sincerely hope that during this meeting I will find a genuine and truthful friend, Ted Ashley.

'As a friend, I am sure you agree with me that, after all, quality, extremely hard work and professionalism is what cinema is all about. My twenty years of experience, both in martial arts and acting, has apparently led to the successful harmony of appropriateness of showmanship and genuine, efficient, artful expression. In short, this is it and ain't nobody knows it like I know it. Pardon my bluntness, but that is me!

'Under such circumstances, I sincerely hope that you will open up the genuineness within you and be absolutely fair and square in our transactions. Because of our friendship, I am holding up my money-making time—like ten offers from hungry producers—to look forward to this meeting. You see, Ted, my obsession is to make, pardon the expression, the fuckingest action motion picture that has ever been made.

'In closing, I will give you my heart, but please do not give me your head only; in return, I, Bruce Lee, will always feel the deepest appreciation for the intensity of your involvement.'

At this stage, he had made up his mind to wait for *Enter the Dragon* to be released to see how it would do. His main concern was to find and work with people of real integrity, for he had been disillusioned by all the phonies who float around on the film scene. His whole drive now, the whole direction of his life was toward the problem of improving the quality of his films; of educating audiences, in particular, to understand that there was a lot more behind kung fu and the martial arts than just plain old fighting. He saw little long-term future for kung fu films or for films of a too-violent nature, really; in fact, he prophesied that the craze for them would not last longer than three years and he saw his own future in terms of greater depth and range as an actor and finally as a director and producer recognizing, in particular, that a martial artist will sooner or later begin to peak out. In the meantime, therefore, while he was waiting for world reaction to *Enter the Dragon*, he worked on the script of *The Game of Death*, preparing to finish it while he considered other offers. At times, I tried to talk him into easing up a little, but he would cut me short by saying, 'The biggest detriment to relaxation is to say: I must relax.' I don't think he would have felt right if he had taken time off to go on a trip or something like that; in fact, I believe it would have been useless to try. For, by this stage, he had convinced himself that he was relaxing when he was working; and I believe that his mind would have been too preoccupied by work problems for him to have enjoyed himself doing something else. I know John Saxon took the view that Bruce's life was just 'spiraling away'; that he had reached a point where he no longer had a goal, that he was just going to go on and on without ever knowing how high he was going. Certainly, he made two contradictory statements in the last months of his life. He said, 'There's no limit, no end in sight, to how far I can ascend in my knowledge of acting and the martial arts'; at the same time, he told me, 'I don't know how much longer I can keep this up.' The strain was there. And the moods were there. I saw his difficulties and I did my best not to add to the stress and strain. For instance, I chose my moments to raise a subject like the kid's schooling or whatever it might be. I didn't burst in and demand his attention about some trivial matter when I knew his thoughts were concentrated on something which was really important. And, whatever the mood, I did not mind, for 'to change with change is the changeless state'.

My world fell apart—although neither Bruce nor I realized it then—on May 10, 1973. It was an intensely hot, intensely humid day. Bruce was working at the Golden Harvest studios, a barn-like structure on Hammer Hill Road, Kowloon. He was busy dubbing the sound to the final print of *Enter the Dragon*. Because of the noise in Hong Kong, all films are shot without sound, which is then dubbed in later and the Concord-Sequoia-Warner production was no exception. In order to prevent extraneous noise from penetrating the dubbing room, there was no ventilation. Usually, the place is bearable enough because of air-conditioning, but while the dubbing was being done that day, the noisy air-conditioning unit had been shut off. The dubbing room was as hot as a ship's boiler room. Bruce, for all the care he took to remain physically fit and for all his vitamins, proteins and juices was, for once, exhausted and weary. The people with him thought he looked unusually tired but, in view of the energies he had expended in his recent film fights and the intensity of the heat, they paid very little attention to him when he left the room. He went into the nearby studio rest room, which was then empty and much cooler. While there, he suddenly collapsed on the floor. He told me later that, to the best of his knowledge, he did not lose consciousness, for he remembers hearing footsteps approaching the rest room and groping around on the floor, pretending that he had dropped his glasses. He got up and walked back into the dubbing room. He was scarcely in the door when he collapsed in a complete faint and lost consciousness. Then he vomited and had an attack of convulsions.

One of the dubbing crew ran to Raymond Chow's office and alerted him that Bruce was ill. Chow asked someone to call a doctor and rushed over to the dubbing room where, he testified before a coroner's jury a few months later, he found Bruce 'having difficulty in breathing. He was making a loud noise and was shaking.' Dr. Charles Langford, a Texan, who runs the nearby Baptist Hospital said that Bruce should be rushed to the hospital immediately. On admittance, Dr. Langford found Bruce unconscious and unresponsive and suffering from a high fever.

By this time, one of the women at the studio had telephoned me: 'Bruce is sick and they're taking him to the hospital,' she said.

'What's the matter?' I demanded.

'Oh, I think it's a stomach upset,' she replied.

It hardly seemed alarming. Indeed, I thought the worst it might be would be his appendix. Or a hernia—he'd had a hernia before. The last thing I considered, certainly, was that it might be a life or death situation.

On arrival at hospital, according to Dr. Langford, Bruce gave 'breathing noises', which then stopped. 'There was a series of convulsions. Three other doctors were summoned, including a neurosurgeon, Dr. Peter Woo.' At this time, Bruce was going through a series of muscle contractions, followed by calm. His body was bathed in sweat—and his breathing was so abnormal that his every breath seemed to be his last. He was literally gasping. His eyes were open at this stage, but they were not focusing. I asked Dr. Langford if he were going to be all right?

'He's very sick,' he replied.

At this stage, Dr. Langford was ready to do a tracheotomy if Bruce stopped breathing. The contractions continued, the entire body being involved in this motion, his arms giving the doctors most trouble because, as Dr. Langford testified, 'he was very strong and difficult to control . . .' When Bruce failed to respond after a while, the neurosurgeon examined him and tests showed that there was something wrong with his brain. 'We gave him drugs (manitol) to reduce the swelling of the brain which we had detected,' said Dr. Langford. The doctors were prepared for surgery at this stage if the manitol didn't work, but, after a couple of hours, he began to regain consciousness. 'It was quite dramatic,' Dr. Langford told the jury. 'First he was able to move a bit, then he opened his eyes, then he made some sign, but could not speak. He recognized his wife and made signs of recognition but could not talk. Later he was able to

195

speak but it was slurred, different from the usual way he talked. By the time he was transferred to another hospital, he was able to remember aloud and joke.' Dr. Woo said a blood test had shown a possible malfunction of the kidney. Bruce was quickly transferred to St. Theresa's Hospital where the facilities were better.

Asked if the symptoms were such as could occur to a person suffering from overwork and exhaustion. Dr. Langford replied, 'No.' He also said that Bruce had seemed near to death.

The doctors wanted to do more tests. Dr. Woo said, 'I was going to examine the brain by injecting a radiopaque medium into it and take a series of x-rays to visualize the blood vessel.' In fact, this was later done by the Los Angeles doctors; Bruce decided he wanted a really complete check-up by the best men in America. Dr. Woo also testified that he had asked Bruce if he had taken any drugs and says Bruce admitted taking cannabis leaf.

Almost the first words Bruce had said to me after he recovered consciousness were that he felt very close to death—but that he could still exert his will and he had told himself 'I'm going to fight it—I'm going to make it—I'm not going to give up' because he knew that if he thought any other way, he would die.

A week later we flew to Los Angeles where a team led by Dr. David Reisbord did a brain scan and brain flow study, as well as a complete physical and an EEG. They found no abnormality in his brain functions—Dr. Langford told me Bruce had suffered a cerebral edema, which is a swelling of the fluid which presses on the brain. There was nothing else wrong with his body. Indeed they told him he had the body of an eighteen-year-old. They finally decided that he had suffered *Grand mal—idiopathic*—which means a type of convulsion due to no known primary cause. The normal treatment for this is to prescribe medication which calms brain activity. Bruce was prescribed the drug Dilantin, but no traces of this were found in his body after death, which seems to indicate that he had forgotten to take it.

196

I should say here that none of Bruce's family ever suffered from epilepsy, even in a mild form; that Bruce had never suffered from it, either. Convulsive fits similar to epileptic fits can be caused by lack of sugar in the blood, lack of oxygen, uremia, injury to the brain from an accident, brain tumors or meningitis. True epilepsy shows no such antecedents—it just happens and, although it is apparently the result of something wrong with the chemistry of the brain, what this something is is not known. Dr. Reisbord told me that at no time had Bruce suffered from epilepsy. Indeed, it is clear to me that he suffered a cerebral edema but what caused it, remains unknown.

While in Los Angeles, Bruce agreed that we would return to America again in August to help promote *Enter the Dragon* and would appear on a series of promotions including the Johnny Carson show.

Back again in Hong Kong, Bruce returned to work on *The Game of Death*. He returned, too, to the usual crop of lurid stories in the local press, some of which linked his name with a young actress from Taiwan, Betty Ting-pei. He also fell out with a local newspaper which ran a series purporting to be by Yip Man's son and which carried some major inaccuracies about Bruce's youth.

I would like to be able to write that Bruce's last days were among his happiest but, regrettably, this would not be wholly true. The film world can be petty and spiteful; with vast sums of money at stake, there are wheels within wheels. As in every business, too, there are personality clashes due to temperament and behavior. For a long time (since his first film in Bangkok), Bruce and Lo Wie, the director had been on anything but good terms. Bruce thought the director too conceited and selfish and a man who simply wanted to 'use' people. Bruce was at the Golden Harvest studios one day talking over ideas for *The Game of Death* with Raymond Chow, when he heard that Lo Wei was in a nearby screening room. As his letter to Ted Ashley shows, Bruce was desperately searching for film men of real integrity and quality to work with; to help him achieve the kind of results that nobody had yet dreamed of. When Lo Wei's name was mentioned—to Bruce his name summed up almost everything that was wrong with Mandarin films—Bruce's hot temper took over and he rushed down to the screening room and in a loud voice let Lo Wei know what he thought of him.

Satisfied at having given vent to his feelings, he returned to Raymond Chow's office. At this stage, the incident seemed at an end. But then Lo Wei's wife appeared and tempers again became heated. By this time —voices had been raised in angry tones—a considerable crowd had gathered. Mrs. Lo went back to her husband leaving Bruce boiling over with anger and frustration. Under normal conditions, he would have quickly calmed down. Instead, he charged back to the screening room and gave Lo Wei another piece of his mind. The director claimed that Bruce had threatened him physically— an absurd claim, of course, but one which was bound to elicit both sympathy and publicity. The police were called and were followed by a horde of reporters. Lo Wei demanded that Bruce sign a paper promising not to harm him physically. Bruce, annoyed and upset by the whole incident and anxious to get the reporters off the premises agreed to sign; later he could have kicked himself, for it appeared to incriminate him. Had Lo Wei been a young man and a reasonable match for him, Bruce's hot temper may well have found an outlet in a fight; but the idea that he would strike or physically injure an old man is beyond credibility.

Bruce was asked to appear on Hong Kong TV that evening and the matter was raised again. Throughout his life Bruce had never feared to state openly and frankly how he felt about people or problems. He was never deliberately rude or deliberately ruthless. He was firm and straightforward, expressing his opinions clearly and unambiguously—which is very different. He did not attempt to conceal his dislike of Lo Wei or his methods, although at no time did he mention the man by his name. In an attempt to show how absurd were sugges-

198

tions that he was prepared to use a weapon against Lo Wei, he decided to demonstrate a simple shoulder push on the interviewer, who was quite agreeable. Bruce put only a fraction of the force he was capable of exerting into the demonstration, but it was still sufficient to look pretty fierce to viewers—and next morning the papers, still seeking for sensation, built up the incident into more headlines. Bruce, in short, had become such a superstar that whatever he did was avidly seized on by the local press. Inevitably, the picture that was presented was a distorted one. It was, very often, a part of the truth—but it was never the totality.

Some of his old friends, such as Stirling Silliphant, hold the view that Bruce, instead of extracting that calmness and tranquility from the martial arts that is part of the teaching of Zen Buddhism, found only conflict and antagonisms. This, of course, is to misinterpret the whole nature of Bruce's philosophy and outlook. Harmony is the interaction of Yin and Yang. In his search for uplift and betterment, for greater and greater achievement, he was following one of the oldest and more constructive forces within mankind, Stirling Silliphant says that Bruce 'invited a lot of these slings that kept coming back at him'. Bruce's answer would have been: 'If you're being criticized, you must be doing something right because they only tackle the one with the ball.'

THIRTEEN

There is not a great deal more to tell; we are now back where we began, with the death of my husband. We are back at that fatal July 20, 1973.

After I had left the house, Raymond Chow duly

called and from about two p.m. until four p.m., Bruce and he worked out a rough script and story for *The Game of Death* to show to George Lazenby that evening. Betty Ting-pei was also to have a leading role in the film and, about four p.m., the two men drove to Betty's flat to fill her in on the details preparatory to meeting George Lazenby at dinner.

At Betty's flat, Bruce appeared quite normal. They all went over the script together, working out more details. Later, Bruce complained of a headache, and Betty gave him a tablet of Equagesic—a kind of super aspirin which had been prescribed for her by her personal physician. Apart from that, Bruce took nothing beyond a few soft drinks. Around seven-thirty p.m., when Raymond was preparing to leave for the restaurant, Bruce complained of feeling unwell and went to lie down in a bedroom. Bruce was still asleep at nine-thirty p.m. when Raymond Chow, who had called at Betty's place to find out why they had not turned up for dinner, returned to her apartment. Bruce, so far as he could see, was still asleep and he saw no signs of convulsions. He tried to waken Bruce by shaking him and slapping his face, but there was no response. Betty at once called her doctor, who came immediately. He, too, found Bruce lying peacefully on the bed. He testified later that he spent ten minutes trying to revive Bruce and then had him taken to the Queen Elizabeth Hospital.

Once the news of Bruce's death broke, of course, the Hong Kong press simply went wild. I could understand the furor. The death of any superstar is newsworthy. One has only to recall the screaming headlines and hysterical scenes that greeted the deaths of young stars such as Rudolph Valentino and Jean Harlow to realize that the death of Bruce Lee at the astonishingly young age of thirty-two was bound to attract the wildest speculation. Had he been a man given to drink and dissipation; had he been killed, like James Dean, in a road accident— even then, I suppose, there would have been much speculation and theorizing. But that a man of Bruce's astonishing virility, vitality, energy and sheer physical fitness should suddenly blank out like a snuffed candle? —perhaps people cannot be blamed for speculating.

The day after Bruce's death, Raymond Chow appeared on Hong Kong TV to talk about it. Part of the resulting confusion was my fault. Raymond had asked if I objected to him making it clear that Bruce had died at Betty's house rather than at home. I said it didn't matter to me—he could do as he thought best. If he thought it better to say that Bruce had died at home, then that was all right with me. We both sensed that the headlines would be larger and more dramatic if the press could link Bruce's name with Betty's. But I really didn't care then and I don't care now—it didn't seem to me all that important, one way or another. I was more preoccupied with thoughts of my children at the time. Raymond did not specifically say that Bruce had died at home, but he implied that he had. When the press found out the truth, it seemed that Raymond had been lying. And if he had been lying, why? The wildest theories and rumors flew in all directions.

The release of the autopsy report did nothing to damp down the sensation of Bruce's death. Traces of cannabis or marijuana were found in Bruce's stomach. The newspapers immediately went to town on the idea that Bruce was a drug addict and had taken drugs to help boost his extraordinary feats. In fact, all the medical evidence given at the coroner's inquiry disclosed that there was no possibility that cannabis, which is a soft drug, could have caused his death. One doctor said that the cannabis was no more significant than if Bruce had taken a cup of tea.

The greatest care was taken to get the true reasons for Bruce's death. A doctor in the Forensic Division of the Hong Kong government laboratory examined the contents of Bruce's stomach and interior organs and other samples were sent to Australia and New Zealand. These disposed of any suggestions of poison or anything of that nature. Apart from a tiny bit of cannabis, the only 'foreign' substance found in Bruce's organs was the

Equagesic. I personally testified that I had only heard of Bruce taking cannabis after his collapse in May, and that I knew that in view of the great care he took of his body and the amount of work he was doing he was not likely to have taken it except occasionally and in small quantities—in fact, Bruce had been told by a doctor that small amounts of cannabis could not possibly do any harm.

Dr. R. R. Lycette of Queen Elizabeth Hospital disposed of the cannabis bogy once and for all when he said that Bruce's death could not possibly have been caused by it. His view was that his system had proved to be hypersensitive to one or more of the compounds in the tablet Equagesic. Some people, for instance, are allergic to penicillin—and the suggestion was that Bruce, in some mysterious chemical way, was not allergic to the drug, but hypersensitive to it. Dr. Lycette also said he had examined Bruce's skull but had found no injuries on it. Bruce's brain, however, was 'swollen like a sponge'. It weighed 1,575 grams against a normal 1,400 grams. But the trouble could not have been a brain hemorrhage because none of the vessels in the brain were blocked or broken. Dr. Lycette said that the brain swelling could have taken place either in half a minute or half a day; in Bruce's case it had occurred 'very rapidly'.

The Crown Counsel, of course, had avidly seized on the cannabis angle as the possible cause of the edema. I submitted a report from Dr. Ira Frank of the School of Medicine at the University of California which stated categorically that nobody in history had ever died of taking cannabis, which had been used by society for thousands of years; the drug was definitely not lethal. Other doctors, having studied the reports and slides of Bruce's autopsy, agreed.

The cannabis theory was completely thrown out by Professor R. D. Teare, professor of forensic medicine at the University of London—and the top expert in the case. He had carried out over 90,000 autopsies and declared that to ascribe the cause of death to cannabis would be 'irrational'. He decided that the edema had been caused by hypersensitivity to either meprobamate or aspirin, or a combination of the two, two of the compounds in Equagesic. However unusual this might be—and cases were rare—this was the only feasible solution. The view was accepted by the jury and a verdict of misadventure returned.

After the verdict, the reporters, as usual, rushed at me, demanding to know if I were satisfied. I could only reply, 'Well, it doesn't really change anything, does it?' For the truth is that from my point of view, all that mattered was that Bruce was dead.

Bruce had two funeral ceremonies—one in Hong Kong and the other in Seattle, where he lies buried. The first was for his friends and fans in Hong Kong—the second was a more private ceremony.

I had decided that Bruce would probably like to wear the Chinese suit he had worn in *Enter the Dragon*; he often wore it casually because it was so very comfortable. I attended the funeral at the Kowloon Funeral Parlour wearing all white, which is the Chinese color of mourning. The casket was not there to begin with, but each person on entering the room walked up to a kind of altar where Bruce's picture was displayed with ribbons and flowers decorating the area and a Chinese banner saying 'A Star Sinks in the Sea of Art'. Three large joss sticks and two candles also burned before his picture. After each person had bowed three times, he or she walked back and took a seat in the body of the hall. When Brandon and Shannon arrived and had donned white burlap robes similar to mine, we sat down on cushions on the floor. Around me were many of Bruce's friends and relatives, including his brother Peter. The Chinese band played a traditional funeral song which sounds like *Auld Lang Syne*. Many famous stars and movie personalities attended the funeral. Outside, the crush was tremendous, and I recalled the old newsreel shots of the funeral of Valentino; there were between twenty and thirty thousand people there. Eventually,

Bruce's casket was brought into the room and positioned near the altar and people filed past the open coffin to see him for the last time. His body was covered with glass to prevent anyone from touching him.

I had decided to bury him in Seattle. I knew that he would prefer the peace and calm of Seattle where the light, fresh rain that he loved so much falls often and there are lakes and mountains and trees all around. I was concerned, too, because the political future of Hong Kong is uncertain and I decided that the day might come when it would not be possible to visit his grave.

Unfortunately, in transit, the casket was scratched. Moisture must have penetrated in some way because when we got him to Seattle, it was discovered that the color from the blue suit had got on to the white silk lining of the casket and we had to replace it. According to Chinese tradition, of course, this meant that he was not resting peacefully.

The funeral in Seattle was a much quieter and more sedate affair. It was attended by some one hundred and eighty friends and relatives. The music was not traditional, but consisted of current songs that Bruce rather liked, including *And When I Die*. The casket was covered with white, yellow and red flowers making up the Yin-Yang symbol. The pallbearers were Steve McQueen, Jim Coburn. Dan Inosanto, Taky Kimura, Peter Chin, and Bruce's brother Robert.

Bruce was buried at Lake View Cemetery overlooking the placid waters of Lake Washington which he knew and loved so well. I said that Bruce had viewed death in the following way: 'The soul of man is an embryo in the body of man. The day of death is the day of awakening. The spirit lives on.' I added that on 'our day of awakening, we will meet him again'. Taky said Bruce had 'inspired good in others'. Ted Ashley spoke of regret at 'what might have been'—of the great future that once lay ahead for Bruce.

Finally at the graveside, James Coburn spoke the last words: 'Farewell, brother. It has been an honor to share this space in time with you. As a friend and as a teacher, you have given to me, have brought my physical, spiritual and psychological selves together. Thank you. May peace be with you.' Then he flung the white gloves he had worn as pallbearer into the open grave and the others followed suit.

I returned once more to Hong Kong for the coroner's inquest. I saw Betty and talked to her and satisfied myself as to what had happened. I realized that it was possible that Bruce had taken Equagesic or aspirin or some other tablet of a similar nature before the attack of May 10; but that whatever was the cause—it may easily have been just some chemistry working within his body—his death had been a natural one. I listened to the fanciful theories and heard the speculations grow; the more closely one analyzed these ideas, the more absurd each seemed. They ranged from suggestions that Run Run Shaw had him murdered to suggestions that Raymond Chow had organized it. The truth was that the Chinese had lost a great hero—and were reluctant to see him die; reluctant to accept that this super-hero, this perfect super-human could succumb as easily as any other mortal. Amid the spate of rumors, counter-rumors and lurid assertions, I publicly pleaded to the people of Hong Kong to let the matter alone: 'The only thing of importance is that Bruce is gone and will not return. He lives on in our memories and through his films. Please remember him for his genius, his art and the magic he brought to every one of us. . . . I appeal to all of you to please let him rest in peace and do not disturb his soul. . . .' No one, I'm sorry to say, seemed to be listening.

I had spent six weeks in Hong Kong attending the inquest, arranging the moving of the house furnishings and so on, and in October I was all set to return to America. I had lived throughout the entire ordeal in a state of semi-numbness. Now, I looked forward to getting away from Hong Kong, away from all the publicity and the rumors, away from an impossible situation—I could not even go out of the house. I was glad, too, to be getting back to Seattle, to my children, to begin facing up to life without Bruce. For six weeks I had been surrounded by friends, by Bruce's relatives, and they had made it as easy for me as possible. I did not feel any sense of injustice; I did not feel that life had been cruel to me—if it had been cruel to anyone, it had been cruel to Bruce. I, after all, had had the happiness of knowing him, of being close to him, of having had nine wonderful, exciting, beautiful years with him.

One of my closest friends, Rebecca Hui, stayed up all night with me before I left Hong Kong. As I say, I had lived throughout these last few months in a state of semi-shock, semi-numbness. I had gone about doing what had to be done as though I were completely normal and controlled. I had tried to carry on as Bruce would have wished me to. I had not broken down nor had I given way to uncontrollable grief. He had relied on me for much throughout our life together—I was determined to continue in the same way.

It was not until I boarded the plane at Hong Kong airport to take me back to America and a new chapter in my life, that the full impact of what had happened suddenly struck home. Everything flooded in as the numbness fell away as though I had been hit by a paralyzing blow, and I was conscious only of the land falling away below me and of the burning tears running down my cheeks.

Then I remembered lines from the ancient Chinese poet Tzu Yeh (A.D. 265-419) which Bruce had translated:

> Young man.
> Seize every minute
> Of your time
> The days fly by;
> Ere long you too
> Will grow old.
>
> If you believe me not

See here, in the courtyard,
How the frost
Glitters white and cold and cruel
On the grass
That once was green.

Do you not see
That you and I
Are as the branches
Of one tree
With your rejoicing
Comes my laughter;
With your sadness
Start my tears.
Love,
Could life be otherwise,
With you and me?

And finally of the words of Jhoon Rhee: 'Bruce was
a man of victory.'

The words of the epi-
taph are Bruce's own
comments on the clas-
sical martial arts.

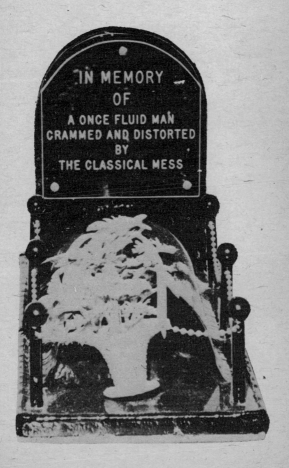

IN MEMORY
OF
A ONCE FLUID MAN
CRAMMED AND DISTORTED
BY
THE CLASSICAL MESS